Hard Target

The Art of Psychological
Self-Protection

By David Oakley

DGO Marketing/Publishing

First published 2020

This edition copyright © David Oakley © 2020

DGO Marketing/Publishing

145 Brighton Road, Worthing, West Sussex BN11 2EU

www.davidoakleymarketing.com

Printed and bound in the United Kingdom

ISBN:978-1-5272-9261-1

Warning

Self-defence is legal. Fighting and being violent towards others is illegal. Make sure you understand the difference or you could end up in prison. The tactics explained in this book, both physical and psychological, are for self-defence. The author and publishers cannot accept any responsibility for proceedings, prosecutions brought or instituted against any person or individual who misuses any techniques or tactics described in this book.

Physical self-protection techniques can only be effectively taught by a professional hands-on qualified instructor. The materials in this book should be used for academic study only.

Dedication

This book is dedicated to my teachers and the men and women who serve their community on the frontline.

Special thanks

Special thanks to all the door staff I worked with who watched my back over the last 15 years and the thugs and villains who tried to take my head off, you all taught me so much.

About the author David Oakley

I have been studying martial arts since the age of 13. Karate was the first martial art I learned and I then went on to train in Wing Chun, Judo, Jujitsu and Boxing. I also competed in Kickboxing in my early years. I have always been fascinated by the far Eastern culture and their fighting arts. Never being one to just accept what I was being told by my peers, I wanted to find out how effective the arts were in real situations. So, I went and worked on the doors as a bouncer for 15 years. Over my time working on the doors, I realised much of what I had learned worked only in a limited way and to be effective had to be applied in a far more practical way. Plus, when it came to real violence, mindset and mental strength were far more important than any type of physical and technical skills.

My conflict management and people skills were honed in casinos whilst working for Caesars Entertainment as a security surveillance officer for many years.

I also have been out on patrols in New York's subways in the Bronx with the legendary Guardian Angels, the original vigilante crime busters who help fight crime in the no go areas of the city.

I am a registered physical intervention trainer and fully qualified conflict management trainer. I have worked in the security industry for over fifteen years. I have also trained hundreds of people in conflict management for real life situations drawing directly from my experience working in mental health, door security and as a surveillance officer for one of the UK's largest casinos.

Level 3 Trainer in conflict management
Level 3 Trainer in Physical Intervention
Level 3 Trainer in First Aid
CPD Training in Personal Safety Awareness
CPD Training in Situational Awareness
CPD Training in Knives and Edged Weapon Awareness

The Art of Psychological Self-Protection

Contents

1. Intro
2. Situational Awareness
3. Techniques for improving your situational awareness
4. The Cooper colour code
5. Boyd's OODA loop and half beat
6. Orientation and your environment
7. Martial arts instructors can be the worst self-protection instructors
8. Trusting your gut instinct
9. Conflict Management
10. Victim selection process
11. Different types of interview
12. Techniques for talking down a potential attacker
13. Safety for students
14. The art of fighting without fighting-de-escalation
15. What will happen to your mind and body when attacked and why   people freeze when being attacked
16. Control the ego
17. Do not push your enemy into a corner
18. Girlfriends can be your worst enemy
19. On the street there are no rounds, rules or referees
20. Self-protection or self-defence?
21. Do not get separated from the herd
22. Does size matter?

23. Learn to spot the little things
24. Positions of attack and ambush
25. Places to avoid
26. Looking through the eyes of a rapist
27. Safety when travelling in the car
28. Safety when travelling on public transport
29. Shopping malls and retail parks
30. Jogging and outdoor exercise
31. Dog walking
32. ATM Cash tills
33. Travelling abroad & backpacking
34. Where is the safest place to sit in a restaurant/café?
35. Knives and edged weapons
36. Knowing the signs when someone is about to hit you
37. The Law and two words you need to understand
38. Can you hit someone first - pre-emptive strike?
39. Working the doors
40. Bank robbers' shotguns and bullshitters
41. Protests and rioting
42. Protecting your teenage children
43. What to do if your teenage children are being bullied
44. Which fighting systems are the best?

Introduction

The world is not the safe place it used to be. Especially in western countries that used to be considered relatively safe compared to many third world regions.

This book is not just about learning to fight or how to overcome someone physically. Real self-protection starts with situational awareness and ends with escape, without ever having to converse verbally or act in any physical way against a potential attacker.

I am writing this book in the year 2020, we are living in strange days indeed. If someone had made a prediction of everything that is going on at this moment in time, they would have been accused of watching or reading too much science fiction. Apart from the Covid-19 pandemic we have rioting, looting, racial tension, gang violence and a population of very frustrated and angry people, due to a widening gap between the have and the have nots in society. I am not going to get into the politics of why this is happening, but my prediction is its only going to get worse.

This book for the benefit of everyone who wants to keep themselves and their family safe, in what is now an increasingly violent society. Many jobs now require people to work out in the community as lone workers, this includes social workers, estate agents, care workers, and door staff, who work one-man doors.

It's not only people who work in the community who are at risk, it's also anyone who goes to and from work, uses public car parks, late night transport or just out for some fun at the weekend in town. Everyone is at risk to the opportunist and devious criminal.

On top of this we have the ever-increasing threat of acts of terror, especially in the big cities. On occasions, aggressive and violent behaviour cannot be avoided and you need to know the best ways to try and deal with it. I will also cover the best courses of action you can take when this happens.

I worked as a bouncer working one-man doors for many years and talking people down from violence was something I had to do on a regular basis. Unfortunately, I did not have the option, that most of you reading this book will have and that is to avoid the situation altogether by spotting the situation before it spots you and taking yourself away from it. This is being what is called a Hard Target.

Please note this book is more about avoiding violence, it is about how to stay safe and not put yourself in harm's way in the first place. Most of this book covers all the skills needed to avoid the physical side of violence; when learning real physical self-protection techniques nothing can replace learning 121 or attending classes with a good self-protection instructor.

When I first started working security, a fight was normally two men or two women having a fist fight. Well, that is not always the case now, especially between males. Knife culture in the UK and Europe is at levels never seen before.

If you get into a fight and there is a knife involved, statistically all deaths from a fight involving a knife come from one single stab wound! I will say that again; most deaths occur from a single stab from a blade.

So next time you are out and you come across trouble in a club or an altercation on the street, steer clear. Unfortunately, a lot of young people like to get involved in other people's drama, trust me it's not worth it. You just do not know what they are carrying on them. Drink, drugs and a knife are a lethal cocktail.

I am not going to bang on about the perils of alcohol and drugs, all I am going to say is this; when you are intoxicated with either, you can make bad decisions. Go out have a good time but keep your wits about you. If you meet someone on a night out, never go back to where they say they live or get in a car with them, and that includes males. The last thing you want after a night out is being accused of something you thought was mutually consensual and was ok to do, while under the influence of drink.

Awareness of predatory behaviour is inherently in all of us. We are programmed to instinctively know when something is wrong. Alcohol and drugs strip that ability away from your senses.

Situational Awareness

Situational awareness is your number one tool in your self-defence toolbox, without it you are flying blind. All human beings and animals are tuned into their environment. It has kept people safe for centuries, the problem is modern times bring many distractions Before modern man, when human beings hunted on the great plains and forests, they were totally tuned into their environment. Because if they were not, they became the hunted and the prey of bigger predators.

When you are walking around with your headphones in your ears and head in the clouds, you become the perfect prey for the opportunist and organised predator who is out looking for prey.

If you look like food, you get eaten!

Because modern life brings so many distractions, we need to retrain ourselves to become more aware of what is going on around us. A simple technique that I use is simply to observe people around me and make a note of what they are wearing, or if they look like a threat: it's a little game you can play with yourself. Do not forget to continually look behind you Someone who is constantly looking about and being aware naturally looks assertive. Remember criminals want easy prey.

No one in their right mind attacks someone who they think will beat them in a fight or looks like they will be a problem to overcome, offer resistance and cause them to get caught in an act of violence or robbery.

Criminals do not want to be caught; they want to complete their objective with as little resistance from their victim as possible. Make yourself a Hard Target by not looking like a victim in the first place.

Situational awareness is not only essential for self-protection and the bad intentions of another person. It is an essential ingredient in everyday life for staying alive or not being severely injured. Many fatal car accidents are caused by drivers simply not being aware of their surroundings.

Take for instance the driver speeding down a side street. The bad driver is only aware of how close his car is to the parked vehicles but the good situationally aware driver is going slower because he's aware that this is a suburban street with the potential risk that children or pedestrians are nearby. Young children have not developed enough awareness or experience to understand the dangers of the road. You, as an experienced and responsible driver, should make allowances to allow for these factors.

US aviation crash investigation experts suspect 80% of most air crashes are down to human error and bad situational awareness.

It doesn't matter if you are flying a plane, driving a car or simply walking down a street late at night. If you have distractions such as earphones, head in a phone looking down at the ground in deep thought about what's going on in your life or simply in a deep conversation with a friend, you are not situationally aware and are putting yourself in potential danger.

Another thing to keep in mind is this, you are most likely to drop your guard in and around the home or place of work; we come and go thousands of times and nothing happens. Stay alert at all times even in familiar places.

Techniques for improving your situational awareness

Be aware of your environment and surroundings.

- Look around regularly and check your surroundings and keep your peripheral vision wide.
- Walk with purpose and confidence as if you know where you are going.
- Never wear headphones when walking or running.
- Do not have valuables on display such as phones or wallets.
- Trust your instincts and gut feelings.
- If you have any doubt or bad feelings of what is ahead, turn around and go back the way you came.
- If you feel scared or threatened go to a public place and call someone or phone the police if it's dark. Make sure you travel in a well-lit area.
- Learn to control your breathing (if you can control your breathing, you can think clearer).

If you are out on the town visiting bars, there are certain times that the risk of violence increases by up to 50%, that's at the end of the evening about an hour before the bars start to shut.

There is an old saying, 'KNOW WHEN TO LEAVE THE PARTY', that way you drastically decrease the risk of violence. Do not go to the town centre taxi rank as the bars are shutting, again this is another area where violence can erupt very quickly and without warning. Believe me on this one. I have worked taxi ranks for years after working the bars and clubs, the very people who were chatting away to me and being friendly in the bar, were trying to punch me in the face on the taxi rank two hours later.

Plan your evening in advance, book a taxi or private hire company to pick you up from outside the venue and always leave well before last orders because if the shit's going to happen this is the most likely time.

The Cooper Colour Code

As a self-protection instructor, I have always taught students and clients the Cooper colour code. Jeff Cooper was a United States marine and is considered the father of the combat mindset and awareness training.

The Cooper colour code is a method to stay alert and be in a constant state of combat readiness.

WHITE Condition white is being totally unprepared and unaware of anything going on around you. If you are attacked while in condition white, the only thing that will save you is being lucky enough to have an attacker who has no idea what he's doing and makes a total mess of whatever he's going to do to you. Condition white is only applicable when you are at home with the doors locked or in a totally 100% safe environment.

YELLOW Condition yellow is a state of low-level constant alertness. You should have situational awareness of what is going on around you in all directions. You should be aware of anyone walking behind you and to the sides and using your peripheral vision, try to spot any potential hidden threats approaching and objects concealing them i.e. alleyways, parked cars, lorries or vans including slow moving vehicles outside of your peripheral vision. Always walk towards oncoming traffic, that way it is more difficult for someone to kerb crawl behind you.

ORANGE Condition orange is something that has come to your attention. It could be a verbal pick up or a visual notification. It could even be gut instinct; you feel something is wrong but you cannot quite work out what it is. Do not ignore gut instinct. Your gut instinct has been honed to perfection through thousands of years of human evolution. Examples of condition orange are overhearing conversations with an aggressive edge to them, suspicious physical activity such as someone trying to be inconspicuous or acting out of character. When taking into consideration of the surroundings and circumstances, cars crawling well below the speed limit, someone laying in the road or pathway in an area with no other people in the area. This is where you should be coming up with answers to the what if.

RED Condition Red is when you must act. This is when you realise the fight is on and action must be taken, such as a first response or pre-emptive strike. This is when you will most likely get hit with the fight, flight or freeze syndrome.

Black Condition black is where you never want to be, it means total cognitive and physical breakdown, this will make you totally inept at defending yourself against single or multiple attackers and could mean certain death. Once the heart rate reaches 140-160 beats per minute, the body feels weak and the conscious brain shuts down giving you virtually no ability to rationalise a way out of danger. Condition black is far more likely to occur if you are in condition white or yellow and then straight into red

It should be noted condition black was not in the original Cooper colour code and was added later by the USMC.

The OODA Loop and the Half-Beat

When John Boyd came up with the OODA loop half beat, it was designed for well-trained military personnel. The OODA loop can be used in the context of situational awareness or actual physical combat. I am not going to go too deep into this as a physical skill because if you are not trained or experienced in actual physical combat, it's not going to be very much used to you.

OODA stands for Observation, Orientation, Decision, Action.

In the book Science, Strategy and War: The Strategic Theory of John Boyd, each one of these elements is briefly explained as follows (in-depth explanations will be revealed shortly):

- **Observation** is sensing yourself and being fully aware of the world around you. This is probably the most important part of the loop. If you make a bad decision here or do not see something that is essential to your safety you could be in a lot of trouble.
- **Orientation** is your belief system: it is a mix of your life filters, personal experience, knowledge, quick evaluation of the situation and confidence to deal with it.

- **Decision** is made by understanding all the information that you have gathered from the first two and concluding the best course of action.
- **Action** is the testing the decision you have made from everything above.

To give you an example, you are walking through a car park late at night, you can see your car at the end of the third floor and there are 4 men hanging around between you and your car.

Observation

You look around you and see there is very few cars in the car park and there is no way you can get to your car without being noticed by the four men. The only three exits from the car park on foot are next to your car, behind you and to the left down a ramp.

Orientation

The only way you can be certain for your safety is to take the exit either behind you or to the left, exit the carpark and call a taxi. *Decision*

Physically turn round and take a safe exit, exit the building, and call a taxi. *Action*

Then keep repeating the OODA cycle indefinitely until you get to a place of safety.

Now, take the above in the context of a physical fight, which you will only be able to do if you are experienced in physical confrontations and combat. What do I mean by half beat? To make things simple in a boxing match, both boxers will be playing out the OODA loop without even thinking about it hundreds of times per minute. Imagine each boxer is fighting at a rate of one move per heartbeat so as an example 2 jabs and 1 hook per 3 heartbeats. The only way to get an advantage over his opponent for one of those boxers would be to move and punch every half beat, in other words you have to fight inside your attacker's loop if you are on the outside of his loop you are just defending. When I worked on the door I was not a knockout merchant or a heavy hitter in a fight, but I made up for it with speed and overwhelming my attacker raining down punches and taking away his OODA loop. In other words, I took away his thinking time and put him on the back foot continually never letting him orientate himself.

Orientation and your environment

Situational awareness is not just about staying safe on the street. Many community care workers, nurses and social service employees must enter buildings with multiple occupants, many with mental health and anger issues. Entering a stranger's property with no knowledge of the layout or who else may be in the building and not knowing where your exit points are puts you at extreme risk.

In the ideal world your employer will have done a risk assessment on the property and gathered all the relevant information regarding the client, they will also have given you GPS tracking and some type of personal alarm system. But let us stop wishing and be realistic, this does not always happen. Don't trust anybody else with the responsibility of your life and safety, make sure you take the responsibility to find out all the relevant information you need and if you can't find it and you feel unsafe, you are perfectly within your rights to refuse to put yourself in potentially dangerous situation. The pressure that is put on nurses and social services to meet targets is a big problem and because of this, corners are cut that can lead you to going into a dangerous environment without even realising you have put yourself at risk.

Martial arts instructors can be the worst self-protection instructors

Martial arts instructors can be the worst self-protection instructors, they confuse martial arts training with self-protection. Trust me I have been a martial arts instructor for over 20 years and martial arts and self-protection are two different things.

One of the main things martial arts instructors forget to teach is situational awareness and conflict management, these two things are more likely to save your life in a dangerous environment than anything else.

Look at it this way, would you get a plumber round to fix your leaky taps or washing machine and then say, 'While you are here can you do all my electrics?' Hopefully the answer to that is no. It is the same with martial arts, just because you have reached a high standard in martial arts, it does not mean you know about self-protection.

To be honest, you really cannot teach self-protection or facts about real violence unless you have been in lots of situations where it has been necessary to practice it for real. Working on the doors gave me a very rude awakening to how effective martial arts were in a real, nasty situation.

Sure, there are elements of martial arts training in self-protection, but martial arts training overall is designed to achieve perfection. Real self-protection is ugly, unfair and a psychological nightmare with no rules. Do not think I am knocking traditional martial arts training because I love it. But I am just being truthful and all martial arts instructors should teach with integrity and truth.

Martial arts are like a big box of skills with many benefits in it. Self-protection is just one of them. If you study martial arts just to get fit and learn punching and kicking techniques, then great. I remember sitting in the cinema watching Bruce Lee films. This amazing man inspired me on my martial arts journey; just remember Lee was one of the first martial artists to teach the truth when it came to competitive competition fighting and self-protection.

If you are a martial arts instructor and teaching the physical elements of self-defence / protection without ever having experienced having to do it for real, then you are doing your students a disservice. Unless you have experienced the adrenaline drop for real and had to fight hard and fast on a good number of occasions, you are no more than a surgeon who's going to perform open heart surgery after learning from a book.

Martial arts are a vocation, a personal journey of self-discovery and lifelong learning. Self-protection is extremely basic in terms of techniques and so-called moves.

But take that as a good thing because good self-protection is academic in nature and considerably basic to learn in any physical way. A good self-protection instructor will teach you a few basic simple moves for any situation. Its 95% mental and 5% physical. On a physical level you need to train with an instructor who makes you feel uncomfortable in every way. Someone who gets your adrenaline pumping.

When I teach martial arts, I make sure the student understands it is just that, a martial art. If they want to learn self-protection then that is a different time, place, and mindset.

In my experience some people cannot be taught the physical self-protection mindset, it is just not in their psyche. But what they can be taught is understanding how the criminal mind works. There are so many things you can do to minimize the risk of becoming a victim, the most important one of all is situational awareness.

Trusting your gut instinct

Over thinking can be very detrimental to us, overthinking can totally disrupt our decision-making process. Have you ever heard of the saying, he or she cannot see the wood for the trees? For many the education system and certain people in the scientific community have been constantly telling us to analyse and be analytic in our thinking because any other method is unreliable and unproven.

But, if you go back only a few hundred years ago, your natural gut instinct and your ability to pick up energy signals was your key to survival.

Intuition or gut feelings are also the result of a lot of processing that happens in the brain. The brain is a large predictive machine, constantly absorbing incoming sensory/energy information and 'in the moment' experiences against stored knowledge and memories of previous experiences as well as predicting what will probably happen next.

Most people, at one time or another, have had an intuitive feeling about something for no reason whatsoever Maybe it was deciding not to walk somewhere and take the car instead for no good reason, just a feeling that that was the right thing to do. How many times have you walked into an office, room or a bar and picked up a bad vibe? Most people have been conditioned to ignore it, that is a big mistake. Intuition and gut feeling are your survival instincts that have been perfected by mother nature for thousands of years.

Working on the doors for 15 years, I lived and survived on my gut instinct and picking up on people's bad energy even before anything had happened. Individuals give off energy, good or bad it is just energy and if you listen to your gut you can pick up on it. There would be certain nights working in crowded bars that the team would be whispering to each other, 'there's something in the air tonight, something doesn't feel right.' Crowds produce far more energy than just one person. Sometimes you could cut the energy in the air with a knife, so to speak, and on every occasion our instincts were proven right. It also worked the other way some nights, however busy, there was just an air of calm energy about them and went smoothly.

Trust your intuition and see it for what it really is: a fast, automatic, subconscious process picking up on the energy that surrounds us. I t can provide us with extremely useful information that deliberate over analysing can't. We need to understand and to accept that intuitive and analytic thinking complement each other and, should time allow in a serious situation, be weighed up against each other in difficult decision-making situations.

Quick Conflict Management guide and check list

If you get caught out and your situational awareness has not kept you out of trouble, then you are into the realm of conflict management.

Does conflict management always work when talking a criminal out of a violent physical or sexual attack against you. The most truthful answer I can give you is, if you are lucky, maybe.

Conflict management skills must be learnt and practiced and you must work out your potential attacker very quickly. Your attacker could have a mental health, drink, or drugs problem. There could be any number of psychological factors that determine the motivations of his or her actions.

Working nightclubs, bars and as a security officer in casinos, I have had plenty of incidents where conflict management techniques have worked well and plenty where they have not. When they did not work, alcohol and drugs were usually the deciding factor for them failing. If I'm refusing entry to someone who's had too much to drink, most of the time they just give you a look with some verbal sparring, a throwaway insult and continue to the next bar. It's important to remember the verbal insults and sparring are word games they are interviewing you to see what you are going to do.

Working as a doorman I could never be seen to back down. There were situations when the casino manager or bar owner has said this person is not allowed in and, on some occasions, I may have thought that to be a wrong decision, but I had to be seen to stick to the original decision. If potentially violent people see you dither or seem unsure about any decision, they will take that as a weakness, a chink in your armour and they will do everything to exploit it. Scumbags and criminals see any act of compassion or kindness as weakness.

For door staff who work one-man doors, it is essential to have a highly skilled conflict management skill set because unfortunately we can't just up and run away, we have to face the aggressor come what may as that's what we have been employed and paid to do.

Most people, fortunately, will have a choice. If your situational awareness was working as it should be. You will have spotted the problem before it spotted you and taken the earliest opportunity to disappear from the scene.

There is always the question if you see something bad going on, such as another person being attacked or breaking the law, should you intervene? This is not an easy question to answer. From my point of view if it is a crime against property then my advice is don't get involved unless it's property on your person or within your property walls. Property can be replaced. If you get stabbed for being a good citizen, is it worth getting yourself killed over an inanimate object?

If it's a crime against the person that's a different matter. If you come across a woman being sexually assaulted, it's completely different to seeing a gang of men attacking someone with knives, you can't help anyone if you are dead. There are many things you can do other than get physically involved and put yourself at risk of being killed.

Calming and talking down a cocaine fuelled thug on a nightclub door is completely different to coming face to face with a mugger or rapist.

Conflict management with a mugger in some ways is quite simple, he wants what you have got. Self-protection is not about winning or losing anything; it is only about getting safely back home. If a mugger has a weapon or not, he's selected you as a victim because he's weighed up the odds and thinks he can dominate you and beat you if push comes to shove, so just give him what he wants.

If it is your phone, wallet, or cash, just give it to him or them, it can all be replaced, you can't be replaced and your survival comes above everything else. If you are lucky, they will take it and run.

A rapist or sexual attacker is a different kind of animal and his motives are completely different. Sexual assaults, generally, are to do with power and control. It would be impossible to cover all the personality traits of a sexual predator but the most important thing is, it's harder to negotiate with someone whose motivation is to dominate and exert their power over you as you are the object of their motivation, not your money or possessions.

When you have been selected as a victim of a sexual attack you have two ways of fighting back. One is to put off the attack in some way such as screaming blue murder and drawing as much attention to the situation as possible. Don't fall into the trap of thinking you can talk your way out of it as the sexual attacker will see this as weakness and capitulation and may even get off on it.

The other option is to fight like hell! 80% of all sexual attacks do not involve a weapon of any type, because if they are caught the sentence is a lot longer, so striking back and making a fight of it is less risky than taking on a mugger. Statistically, with assault and robbery, there is a much more likelihood of there being a weapon involved. Of course, that is no guarantee that there will not be a weapon in a sexual attack, no two attacks will ever be the same.

So just to reiterate and make the point.

Assault and muggings carry a much more increased likelihood of a knife or weapon being involved.

Give them what they want and do not increase the risk of injury or death by trying to protect something that can be replaced.

Trying to talk your way out of a sexual assault and thinking you can negotiate your way out of trouble is probably not going to work and may even encourage the attacker.

If you get the chance make as much commotion and noise as possible to bring attention to what going on. The more you scream and make a ton of noise the more chance of your attackers fight or flight response being activated, the last thing your attacker wants is to be caught. You have to look at it from a rapist's point of view. The sexual attacker's motive is to sexually assault you, to do that is going to take a certain amount of time so you have to psychologically take away his time which will cause him to question his chances of getting caught.

Sexual assault within a relationship creates safe time and safe space for the sexual attacker. This is a far more complex issue and deserves its own book. This book concentrates attacks by opportunists and total strangers.

Techniques for dealing with conflict

This section is for people who work in conflict or potential conflict environments such as community, healthcare or social workers.

Dynamic Risk Assessment

"A method of continuously assessing situations to ensure that risks of violence

are quickly recognised, assessed and responded to"

A conscious and reliable process.

A dynamic risk assessment is making sure you have an absolute awareness of any potential threat going on around you in real time. In other words, don't assess the situation then relax and stop being situationally aware of everything around you; stay sharp.

SAFER

STEP BACK. Don't just rush into a situation blindly without looking and seeing exactly what is going on. Do not just focus on the point of conflict or the centre of your attention. This doesn't even have to be a conflict situation; it could be as simple as somebody laying on the kitchen floor face down not moving. A typical reaction would be to go and tap them and roll them over to see if they are OK. Not a good idea if they have been electrocuted and are still in contact with a cable or loose wire. No matter how fast you think you should act, if you are dead you won't be helping anyone.

ACCESS THREAT. When you have looked at everything going on, ask yourself is this something I can deal with or is this a situation that I have to remove myself from a personal safety point of view.

FIND HELP. If possible, before entering any situation, alert someone either by verbal communication i.e. shouting, calling out or calling someone on the phone, before you think of entering any type of situation especially buildings or dodgy areas at night.

EVALUATE OPTIONS. Now you can decide a course of action, it could mean you proceed with the situation or it could mean, after assessing the situation, waiting for a police presence or back up from a colleague.

RESPOND. Responding to the situation either by going forward or leaving until help arrives.

This should be a continuous process (Dynamic)

When working in potential conflict environments many workers have previous experience with difficult service users and patients or in the case of nightlife security, they have previous encounters with villains and troublemakers.

A useful guide is the term **POP**

POP

PEOPLE

OBJECT

PLACE

Pre-cues to violence

Here are a number of things that may indicate that a conflict situation may be about to shift up a gear and become physical.

- Scanning the environment.
- Witness, his mates, escape.
- Target glance – YOU
- Clenching- Teeth, Jaw, Hands, Colour drain from the face.
- Rapid blinking or significant stare or slowdown of blinking.
  It's called the thousand-mile stare or looking through you.
- Significant sign of immediate attack shifting of weight on to
  one leg usually the one behind.
- Flanking in multiples.
- Slow repose to any questions you ask them.
- Posturing – dominance.

Situations and reasons that can turn people to physical violence

What turns people to violence?

Violence

Aggression

Anger

Frustration

REDUCING FRUSTRATION

- Be proactive
- Give the person getting frustrated room and an escape route, both physically and psychologically
- Provide communication and help them understand why and what's going on
- Responding to their questions and complaints seriously

- Managing their expectations
- Explaining any rules and why decisions have been made in a none condescending way
- Use effective communication and simple language. Don't use clever or condescending words. When someone is frustrated or angry, they have limited understanding of complicated language.
- Make sure that they understand what you are trying to convey to them.

The difference between body language, words and tone of voice.

As a person becomes more frustrated and angrier, their ability to understand word rapidly diminishes. Once a situation becomes heated, non-verbal signal become far more important to resolving and cooling down the conflict escalation into violence.

- **Body language accounts for 55% of communication when under stress**
- **Tone of voice accounts for 38% of communication when under stress**
- **Words account for only 7% of communication**

Blocks to good communication

- Background noise
- Heat, pain, hunger
- Language
- Drinks/drugs
- Mental illness
- Culture
- Emotion
- Attitude
- Psychological noise
  Your behaviour affects every situation

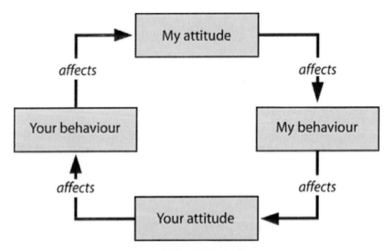

Your behaviour is everything you do and everything you say. When I worked in casino security, I found that I could control most situations with words, not physical force or fists.

First impressions count.

Uses active listening

Really listen to what they are saying

Focus your attention on them

Use non-verbal clues

Paraphrase, make it clear as you can

Use 'open' questions to engage a conversation

Triggers to violence

We need to avoid accidently 'triggering' someone to showing violence towards us

A 'Trigger' is something that causes someone to lose their temper and turn to violence.

- **Embarrassment**
- **Disrespect**

- **Insults**
- **Rudeness**
- **Being ridiculed**
- **Being ignored**
- **Being patronised**
- **The victim selection process**

Inhibitors

An 'Inhibitor' is something that stops someone from losing their temper and turning to violence

- **Social or legal consequences of their actions**
- **Self-control**
- **Personal & moral values**
- **Fear of the other person fighting back.**

- **Building a quick relationship with the person. This can include a compliment.**

One that I use regularly in a suspect situation is to compliment something such as a tattoo and ask where they had it done. It's harder to be violent towards someone you have any type of relationship with.

Fight or Flight

Do not trigger a person's fight or flight emotions.

- **Reasons for fight or flight.**
- **Intimidation**
- **Touching**
- **Standing to close**
- **Inappropriate gestures (signals)**
- **Blocking their exit or cornering them**

Managing a conflict situation is all about engaging the rational brain. When a person is angry and upset, it's because the emotional side of their brain has taken over and pushed back the rational brain. The longer you can keep a person engaged in verbal communication the more chance you have of avoiding violence.

When a person is angry and upset, adrenaline is being dumped into their system but this only lasts for a limited time. The longer you can keep someone talking, the more chance you have of bringing back the rational side of their brain.

Other Signs of Escalation

- Staring (or very strong eye contact)
- Frowning
- Flushed red face (colour might drain nearer to an attack)
- Stepping in and invading personal space
- Pointing, gesturing or head thrust forward to invade personal space
- Standing 'square on'
- Splaying the arms to make themselves look larger
- Turning to one side into a 'fighting stance'
- Making a fist
- Looking at the area they are intending to strike
- Pupils dilate
- Rapid heavy breathing
- Rapid hand and body shifting movements
- Offensive words.

If you look like food, chances are you will get eaten.

How you walk and how you present yourself out in the streets has a big influence on whether you get picked as a victim by an opportunist attacker or passed over for someone else who looks like easier prey.

As I said earlier, no-one in their right mind attempts to assault or mug someone who looks as if they are going fight back hard.

Working on one-man doors, playing poker and mind games was a big part of the game. I am not a violent thug who wants to fight and do serious damage to anyone, I am fundamentally a peaceful person who just wanted to get home in one piece at the end of the shift. But on occasion I had to become a chameleon and present myself as a violent individual with no morals to put off potential attackers.

Unless out of their mind on drugs, most thugs will not go near someone who they think can dominate and beat them in a head-to-head punch up.

If they can help it, muggers or thugs do not pick fights with people who will pound them into the pavement! They will not select people who look like they will confront and challenge them. Rapists, muggers, abusers and bullies look for someone they can dominate and control with ease.

Different types of interview

The silent interview, this is the interview you are totally unaware of, you are going about your business totally unaware you are being watched and being weighed up as a potential victim. This is where your body language decides if you are safe victim potential. Human predators select their prey based on signals given off by their potential victims.

The predator acquires a sense of who is and is not a suitable target. For every person who is a victim, ten others are passed over.

How you walk - People selected as victims can have an either abnormally short or long stride. They drag or shuffle their feet as they walk. Non-victims, on the other hand, tend to have a smooth, natural walk. walking from heel to toe.

Assertiveness when walking about - Victims tend to walk at a different rate than non-victims. Usually, they walk slower. Their movement lacks a sense of deliberateness or purpose. However, an unnaturally rapid pace can project nervousness or fear.

Body control - Awkwardness or lack of co-ordination in a victim's body movement. Wavering from side to side as they moved became apparent in all the victims who were analysed. Compared with smoother, more coordinated movement of the non-victims.

Posture and eye contact, A slumped posture is a sign of weakness or being submissive. A downward gaze implies preoccupation and being unaware of one's surroundings. Reluctant to establish eye contact can also be perceived as being scared or submissive, an ideal target for a predator.

The sudden interview. This is the type of verbal interview that happens suddenly and is full of verbal abuse from the moment it starts. For the untrained person this is very frightening, it's designed to overwhelm you and make you capitulate and submit before you can start to think straight.

If not quickly handled this normally escalates quickly to a physical level. It's very important that you act quickly and decisively by creating distance between you and the attacker, keep your hands raised and stare back at them straight in the eye, make it clear you are not going to be an easy target.

The escalating interview. This type of interview is a gradual process, remember the frog in boiling water? If you throw a frog into boiling water it will immediately jump out. But if you put the frog into normal temperature water and gradually turn up the heat it will boil to death. So be cautious and be very switched on from the beginning of any type of heated discussion.

The crafty interview. This could be something as simple as asking for directions, stopping you and asking for a cigarette or change, quite often this is a multiple attack with someone you have not even noticed lurking nearby. It is especially important when stopped by anyone no matter how innocent they look, to keep a safe distance.

If they close the distance keep your hands up in an open palm gesture and move slightly back keeping out of striking range. Keeping your hands up above theirs may make you feel awkward or over reactive, this is normal. You will feel a lot more awkward if you have to stop or try and avoid a surprise

.h that's in perfect range of your chin. The professional
_ eet criminal or predatorial sexual attacker will use any
number of slimy manipulative sneaky ways to take away your
guard.

When dealing with any of the types of the interviews above, it
is essential to keep your hands above the hands of the
potential attacker.

In the world of bouncing, understanding the fence is the bread
and butter of staying safe in any potential interview process. A
good Doorman/Bouncer will use the fence technique when he
is talking to you and you will not even realise he is lining you up
and ready to put you on the floor. I could write a book just on
the fence, it is an art all on its own. In the back of this book
there is a link to my YouTube channel where you can see how
the fence is employed in detail.

Techniques for talking down a potential attacker.

The longer you can keep someone talking, the more chance you
have of calming them down. Initially they will be fuelled up on
adrenaline, shutting down their rational brain and priming
them for fight or flight. Chances are if they are in your face, it is
a fight they are looking for.

If you can keep your distance and keep them talking the
adrenalin in their system will quickly wear off, which in turn will
switch on the rational brain. This works well depending on

other factors such as drugs, alcohol or types of mental illness. The other major factor can be peer pressure. If they have a bunch of mates spurring them on, they get to a stage of feeling they cannot back down.

Working on the door I had loads of techniques in my toolbox for talking people down. I could control what certain individuals did by just using my hands in a deceptive way as a fence and communicating with people in certain ways, enabling me to switch off their aggression at will. From a physical point of view the fence acts as a very deceptive defence mechanism enabling you to defend or attack.

As I have said before, an experienced doorman can work from the fence position. After a few years they can develop a keen sense of what someone is going to do exceedingly early on in any potentially violent confrontation and positions themselves accordingly.

Safety for students

If you are studying away from home, it is an exciting time starting out as a resident student. With most students it's all work and lots of fun, I expect mum and dad have told you to be careful and watch out for this and watch out for that. I expect you won't take any of it very seriously, because all you can see is fun times ahead.

There is nothing wrong with having a good time and making new friends. But in amongst all this fun there are many dangers especially when you are in a new town or city and you are not familiar with the area. Criminals and sexual predators have hunting grounds and where better to hunt than young people who have come from a different area and may not know aspects of the location/ environment or unscrupulous characters that exist in the area.

I have taught self-protection to many college and university students, and the thing that they all have in common, especially young males, is that they don't realise what kind of people are out there and think that they themselves are indestructible should violence ever pay them a visit. Do not get me wrong I was just the same, at 18 years old I thought nothing could hurt me or kill me.

Knife crime mainly affects the age group of 17-25 and the reason for that is the no fear factor. The no fear factor is why young men are happy to join the army and go off to an area of conflict, they honestly believe they are indestructible.

Young girls are also vulnerable especially when it comes to drink spiking or simply drinking too much. As I mentioned earlier when under the influence of alcohol, unwise or simply bad decisions can be made.

Here are a few simple tips.

- Check out where you are going to be staying both during the night as well as daylight hours, does it feel safe? Are the streets well-lit? Are there any busy bars nearby? Is it very secluded and off the beaten track?

- If you are staying in university camp residence on site, never let strangers in through the front door if they do not have a passcode, key, or live there. Always keep your door shut and locked if you leave your room, never leave the door ajar to visit a friend down the hallway.

- Never invite strangers or people you have met on a night out into your room, monsters never reveal themselves until it is too late. I cannot say this enough; do not trust anyone you have just met or do not know, even if they are a friend of a friend. Do not even invite them into the building as you are not only putting yourself at risk but also everyone else in the building.

- As I have said before always trust your gut instinct, if you are house sharing and house mates bring in guests, try and make sure that you all lay some ground rules before inviting people back and always have a lock on your door to your room when house sharing.

- Make sure all your housemates keep the house secure and make sure doors are locked and windows are shut when they leave the premises.

- Do not keep access cash in your room or lots of valuable goods such as laptops and luxury brand items on show.

- Always keep a personal attack alarm on you.

- Always plan your evening out and decide how you are getting back and if possible, never walk home on your own. Stay with friends at all time if possible.

- Always book a taxi from the venue back to your residence.
- Never give out personal information to strangers when you are out, especially where you are staying. Not only do you put yourself in danger but you also put your room mates in danger too.
- When you are travelling about, always walk towards the oncoming traffic. It's much harder for someone to slow down or stop to bother you, plus you can see if a car starts to slow down near you.
- Stay aware always. Do not use headphones or have your face stuck down looking at a phone screen.
- If you are traveling by public transport always make sure you know when the last train or bus is running.
- Keep your mobile fully charged and install local taxi numbers and roommates' numbers.
- Make sure you have money (cash) left over at the end of the night in case of emergency and keep cash and credit cards separate.
- Never accept drinks from strangers or go home with them or invite them back to yours after a night out!

The art of fighting without fighting or de-escalation

A couple of techniques that worked well for me on the door when faced with an angry drunk threating to do me damage was to get into a conversation that would reveal what they did for a job. One time I had a brain-dead drunken thug asking if I was going to stop him by force getting into the bar and would I be up for a fight about it. This was a one-man door so no back up apart from the landlord who at that time was busy behind the bar. My reply was if that was what it required, that is what I would do. He just looked at me and grinned and started to push forward.

I raised my hands to the fence position to stop him but at the same time started a conversation about what he did as a job and I could see his brain trying its best to do a right-hand turn. Eventually he replied 'a kids football coach,' I grinned back and said 'Don't you need a CRB/DBS check for that? What's going to happen when the police turn up after the fight?' I just wish I could have photographed the look on his face, all I needed was Noel Edmonds to turn up with a gotcha to have made it perfect. Guess what? He moved back, whispered a few insults and went off with his tail between his legs.

A perfect example of the famous Bruce Lee quote; The art of fighting without fighting.

Another one that worked well was a technique I called softening the potential target before anything happened. After years working the door you know who's likely to kick off just by looking at them and sensing their bad energy. I could look at some people and I would think 'ok, in 30 minutes I will probably be asking him to leave,' or her on some occasions. So again, the first chance I would get, I would chat to them. It could be simple stuff like 'Where did you get your tattoo done? I t looks great.' Or 'What did you do today?' Here is the thing; any positive conversation forms a relationship no matter how shallow. So, when it came time to ask him or her to leave, there is a history of conversation/relationship behind the tension, usually just enough to stop them becoming physical and trying to punch me in the face.

Another thing I used to do would be to change the context of the argument. If, for instance, there was a dispute at the bar or an argument between two other customers, I would be called upon to remove one or two people from the premises or at least resolve it before it got to the point of being physical. It does not take long for a heated argument to turn into a full-scale punch up so fast communication is essential. I would take one of them to one side, usually the one who I suspected of being the aggressor and instigator of the incident, and empathise with his point of view but point out that there were CCTV cameras around the bar, or above the cash till, if it was a payment dispute. Pointing out the fact that something could be used in evidence in a court case or a night in a cell was usually enough to discourage violence.

The key to de-escalation is empathy or at least pretending you understand their point of view.

It didn't always work but working the door is a game of percentages. I only used to fight when I had to and when I did, I had a clear conscience to use everything in my toolbox to win the fight.

If you think you are hard and a good fighter, chances are you are not! Over the years working on the door, I have seen many so-called hard men be made fools of when it comes to a walking the walk. In my experience there are walkers and talkers, people who can do not go around saying they can.

There is no truer saying, it is the quiet ones you must watch. I do not care if you are a local title holder in boxing, MMA or any other martial art, there is always someone tougher than you. A wise man shuts his mouth and observes the situation, a smart man will be gone before it ever gets to this point in the first place. The egotistical man is usually the one who ends up in hospital.

I can't emphasise enough there are people out there who will really try to hurt you, they don't have the same moral code of conduct that you have, to them life is cheap; stamping on your head or pulling out a knife and stabbing you is no big deal.

When it comes to real nasty violence, it really isn't down to fighting skills in the end, surviving real violence comes down to one very big factor, are you prepared to go further down the dark tunnel of violence than your attacker and bring a greater degree of violence to the table than they are?

The really dangerous people out there are not your MMA fighters, boxers or self-defence instructors, they are the street scum, psychopathic individuals that have no moral values, life is cheap they have no fear of the consequences of their actions, they don't care if they cause life changing injuries or kill you and they don't care if they are caught and sent to prison.

In truth, most of you reading this will not be able to step up to this level of mental and psychotic behaviour, very few people can which is why it's best to understand the psychology of the criminal mind and understand personal safety and situational awareness to avoid getting into such a dire situation with these types of people in the first place.

One of the main reasons for the average person not to take on an experienced violent street criminal is the fact they are going to be a lot better than you at violence, not something you want to hear maybe but it's the truth. Even if you are an experienced competition fighter the chances are you won't go to the depths of depravity a street criminal will sink to in order to get a winning outcome. Remember this, most effective street fighters and murderers have never trained in any martial art or fighting system. They will beat you with their lack of any type of compassion, morals and pure unrelenting violence.

What will happen to your mind and body when attacked and why people freeze when being attacked.

When you are faced with danger your natural body defences kick in automatically, most people are not used to any type of violence on a regular basis, so unless you work in conflict situations facing verbal physical assaults regularly your body will kick in a more extreme version of fight or flight than someone who is used to it.

It's bad enough when you are used to it but after a time dealing with violence, you become desensitised to it and the physical and mental effects do not affect you in such a negative way.

For most people, the first thing that happens is a dramatically increased heart rate. It can increase as much as 220 beats per minute and once above 150 beats per minute, your ability to function cognitively and physically are severely impaired.

From 160 beats and above the first things are auditory exclusion, loss of near vision and loss of peripheral vision (tunnel vision). Understanding why this is happening is essential if you want to keep things under control, most people do not understand why they are feeling this way, they just know the feeling as being scared but it's no more than your body preparing you so you have the maximum chance of survival. That butterfly feeling in your stomach and the sudden urge of wanting to go to the toilet is all part of the process of fight, flight or freeze.

The reason your stomach gets butterflies is the fact that a massive amount of adrenalin has been dumped into your system and the blood being pumped from your stomach to your arms and legs, preparing you for a fight or running away.

As this happens you will also lose most of your fine motor skills, hence most complex fighting skills will have deserted you and will be nowhere to be seen. This is the reason I teach all my self-protection students gross motor skills, not fine motor skills.

It's because of all the above, it's more or less impossible to fight and win against a seasoned street thug unless you have actually immersed yourself into realistic fighting scenarios such as hard free sparring in sports such as boxing, knockdown karate or MMA. Even that won't guarantee your safety and ability to get away as in any combat sport there are rules. When it comes to street criminals, muggers and rapists, they have no rule book to adhere to.

Between 180-2020 heartbeats per minute causes total loss of coordination, vasoconstriction (the body constricts blood flow as a failsafe mechanism in extreme danger), light headedness and total freeze up and the complete inability to defend yourself.

The only way of combatting this is by slowing your breathing down as much as possible, by controlling your breathing you can slow the heart rate. But if you have no experience in a violent physical conflict situation this is going to be far harder than you know and to the average person, probably unachievable.

Once you reach 140-160 beats per minute your conscious brain shuts down and your primal brain and instincts kick in, you will not be able to stop millions of years of human evolution.

The part of the brain known as the *amygdala* overrides most other brain functions and sends a message to the adrenal glands and floods the body with adrenalin.

Adrenalin kicks the heart into action. Imagine Nitrous Oxide being pumped into the fuel system of a sports car, it speeds everything up and makes it go faster.

The plus with adrenalin is that it makes you faster, it gives you the ability to move quickly, it makes you stronger and heightens your senses to the danger around you and acts as a pain killer.

The problem with anything that goes too fast is the ability to control it becomes far more difficult. If the heartbeat reaches 190 plus, it can lead to total freeze or at worst loss of consciousness.

Below is a brief explanation why women freeze and do nothing when sexually attacked. The key to combatting a sexual attack is first understanding why you feel the way you do. It has nothing to do with a conscious decision not to fight back.

The amygdala is part of the *limbic* system of the brain (commonly known as the reptilian brain) This part of your brain controls your survival instincts and activates your adrenaline dump into the body, your cognitive brain is your conscience. Think of the limbic system as your hard drive and the cognitive brain as the software to develop certain thought patterns and skillsets. The problem is when you are in a situation of extreme threat, physical and emotional, the amygdala hijacks and shuts down the cognitive brain and activates your primal instincts so basically you only have use of the limbic system of your brain (the hard drive) when being sexually or violently attacked.

The little bit of cognitive thinking you have left will search the limbic system for a solution. Your survival instincts, having kicked in, will do whatever it takes will ensure your survival. If there is no solution within the limbic system, you will do nothing (freeze) because it has no experience in your data banks for a solution.

So, when you hear people asking, 'Why she did not fight back and do nothing when she was being raped?' it is because the only thing in her limbic system memory banks was nothing. So that is exactly what she did, nothing. Her survival instincts told her doing nothing was her best chance of survival.

The only way to implant a solution into the Limbic system is to train to a real as possible real-life scenario so that an emotional response is activated. An emotional response will cause an adrenaline dump and the two together will be like installing software into the sub-conscience mind (limbic system) so when it happens for real, when your survival instincts kick in, it has an experience/solution to draw on.

This is the reason you need to train with an experienced self-protection instructor if you are going to learn to protect yourself, a martial arts instructor who has no experience of real-life conflicts and fights will not cut it.

Control your ego

Escaping from violence may not sound like a cool thing to do but it is the only sensible option to take.

Do not get yourself severely hurt or killed because you could not keep your ego under control. When it comes to young people mixed with testosterone, alcohol or drugs, or all three, it's like adding petrol to a fire and makes it impossible to keep a cool and rational head when the shit hits the fan. If you can walk away then walk away, better to have a bruised ego than a knife you didn't see puncture your lung or sever an artery. You only die once.

Do not push your enemy into a corner

This is a famous quote from Sun Tsz (The Art of War) Always leave an escape route for your enemy. This could be in a physical sense or a psychological sense, better to use the latter as it might save you from getting badly hurt. Working bars and pubs on my own with maybe 100-150 people, I realised you must work smart or it will not be long before you are in a world of trouble. From a physical point of view, it means when you are winning the battle and your enemy is in retreat, don't push them into a corner without a way out because a desperate enemy with nothing to lose will do the most damage to an opposing army when cornered with no way out. In a street situation know when to back off, if it looks like your aggressor is going to give up and leave the situation, give him the room to get away and if possible, let him save face in the process. In other words, manage his ego to your advantage.

From a psychological point of view, this could be some guy in a bar who has had too much to drink and giving it large, and he must be asked to leave. There are two ways this can be achieved, peacefully or a full-blown punch up; as I worked on my own in many bars I always tried the peaceful way first.

All human beings need to feel respected, if you make someone look stupid in front of their mates or girlfriends it's going to put their backs up and give them an urgent need to level the situation in the eyes of their friends or lovers. So, I would pull them to one side, out of earshot of friends, and politely explain they had had enough and when they had finished their drink they would have to leave. If they did go nicely, they would be welcome to revisit the bar another time. By doing this I had given him two important gifts; one, he could leave the situation without being forcibly removed from the premises so all he had to do was say to his friends or girlfriend 'let's go and visit another bar or whatever story he wanted to tell them. Two, there was no problem with him and his friends coming back on another evening which made it clear it was nothing personal about my decision. Eight times out of ten this would work perfectly.

In a nutshell, give people respect and do not make them look stupid you will save yourself a lot of trouble in the process.

Girlfriends can be your worst enemy

Some girls get a massive turn on watching you fight for them; I have seen it so many times. I have seen girls cajoling their boyfriends to fight over something stupid and it goes back to tribal times when females were picking a mate, they would want a strong assertive warrior type so seeing if he's willing to fight for her honour some girls will happily encourage their potential mate to fight for them without thinking of the consequences.

If you have a girlfriend like this, then it is time to ditch her for someone else. A girl with this type of personality will be trouble for as long as you are with her, get rid and let her be someone else's problem.

I have known girls who are out with their boyfriends purposely start flirting with other males in the club or bar, literally doing everything they can to get a fight going. I can tell you now this type of girl is going to get you seriously injured or you ending up in a prison cell.

A typical one for me to deal with, would be a couple coming to the door with one, or both, having had one too many to drink and being refused entry. First it would be the female getting in my face and then she would maybe try to push past. I would hold my hand up to which she would then accuse me of being physical with her, then step back and egg the boyfriend to defend her honour by challenging me to a fight.

The difference is, when they did it to me the boyfriend was aware I was probably a seasoned bouncer and had had a few fights and the odds on him coming out on top were slim. Now, let us just say she had done that inside the bar with another guy who was not as big as me and did not look as much of a threat when it comes to fighting back. Some of the most pathetic looking creeps out there carry knives. Do not think because someone does not look like a fighter, he will not pull out a blade and stick it in you. Scumbags come in all shapes and sizes.

On the street there are no rounds rules or referees

I have seen people get knocked out cold with one well-placed punch, it is not the sound of the punch that is frightening it is the sickening sound of the head hitting the pavement. Once you have been knocked out you are totally at the other persons mercy, relying on their self-control not to start stamping on your head.

I can tell you from experience, it's extremely easy to go beyond the realms and lawful limitations of self-defence when in an adrenalized state. I know, I have been there. When the adrenaline starts pumping and you have the upper hand in a physical fight, the adrenaline drop rushing through your body is the equivalent of having no brakes on a 200-mph supercar.

A street fight is never fair; there's no rounds, no referee, no rules and cheating is a must, even if that means hitting someone from behind with a brick, laws are written by people who will never live in the same world that the average person has to live in. Those very same people will never be in your corner when you need them to come to your aid in a violent encounter.

The only person who will protect you in any violent situation is you and you alone. You are the one who must take responsibility in learning everything you need to know about keeping you and your family safe and that includes the physical and the mental side of self-protection, the police and emergency services will not be there when you need them, they only appear after the facts.

Most of this book covers the mental side of self-protection but if you can learn physical self-protection from a genuine instructor who has worked in door security, close protection or is military trained, I strongly advise you to do so.

Remember it is much easier to negotiate a peaceful solution in some situations if you have a shotgun up your sleeve.

When it comes to finding an instructor, don't just go to the first one you find, search around and watch. If someone is calling themselves a master or claiming to teach secret ancient killer techniques or tells you that their system is the best, run a mile. Make sure your bullshit detector is fully switched on because when it comes to the self-protection industry, the bullshit is waist deep.

My advice to martial arts instructors who want to teach self-protection is to go and work as a night club/bar doorman, even if it is for only a few years. You can only teach what you have had real experience of. I only suggest working as a doorman because this is where you are going to get lots of practice dealing with confrontations and coping with violence directed at you on a regular basis. Not only will it give you far more credibility with clients and students but more belief in yourself and what you are teaching.

Self-protection or self-defence?

I try to use the term self-protection rather than self-defence as for me, self-protection suggests a more positive pro-active approach to staying safe, rather than a reactive mindset suggesting you are on the backfoot from the start. If you are fully aware of your surroundings, you are not being reactive or passive to the dangers going on around you.

Do not get separated from the herd

Have you ever watched lions and tigers hunting their prey? They very rarely attack the inside of the herd, they look for the stragglers, the young, the vulnerable; human predators are no different. When you are out on the town or in an unfamiliar environment, make sure you stay well within the view and range of as many other people as possible. Do not go exploring quiet parts of town especially when in other countries, towns or cities you do not know.

A perfect example is when I was in New York and visiting the areas like the Bronx or Brooklyn. You do not go asking strangers for directions or where this or that is, you are basically saying you don't know the area and are a tourist, it's the quickest way to get mugged. Get out of the habit of thinking it will not ever happen to me. I would even go as far as saying go about you daily life expecting it.

Does size matter?

It is an interesting question. There is an old saying it is not the size of the dog in the fight but the size of the fight in the dog. Don't get embroiled in a confrontation with someone and push the envelope of aggression; just because someone is smaller than you or slightly built it doesn't mean they won't be able to beat the shit out of you. Now that said, if you have the right attitude with a large attacker then the same goes for you, so don't think you can't deal with a violent encounter just because your attacker is larger than you. When it comes to the physical side of self-protection, we have all the same weak and vulnerable areas.

That said, a slightly built female is no match for an average built aggressive male unless you have a toolbox full of dirty tricks, you are willing to use them and more importantly have experience in using them. If you, as a female, use your primary weapons such as fists, elbows and feet against the same set of weapons of a male attacker nine times out of ten you are going to lose. A woman will need to use secondary weapons such as nails, teeth, fingers and go for soft targets such as the eyes, ears and groin and, if really in trouble, bite and spit out flesh as a means to stay alive.

If you are about to be raped ask yourself the question, would you be prepared to bite your attacker's ears or nose off or poke your thumb with a nice sharp nail into an eye or two?

Any women that come to me for self-defence training go through high intensity training drills with me taking them to the floor and simulating an attack as realistic as possible. I wear full head gear with eye holes so they can use every weapon I have shown them to get me off, one woman actually bit my chest as she was so far in the zone, I have never moved so quickly in my life to get away. If you are going to prepare yourself physically and mentally for a real fight for your life you must train as near as possible to the real thing. Afterwards women, and men for that matter, tell me they feel mentally exhausted, I really make my students feel as uncomfortable as possible. On a three-hour training course, I'm not friendly until the end. I'm very matter of fact, swear a lot and do everything I can to disorientate and upset them as well as make them wish they hadn't signed up. Because that is nothing compared to a real situation.

Learn to spot the little things

In most aggressive encounters you will be focused on the face of your aggressor but do not forget to keep your eyes peeled for other clues and bad intentions, such as the hand in the pocket or slightly hidden behind their back. ALWAYS THINK WEAPON and keep a safe distance.

As hard as it may be, try to be aware of what is going on in your peripheral vision as you never know if they have accomplices ready to flank you. Even walking down the street, look left and right and behind as often as possible. Working the door, I have met and chatted to many victims of crime. One poor guy was just standing outside a venue and out of nowhere he was headbutted which resulted in a broken eye socket and two metal plates in his head. He was just picked at random, there was no previous with the attacker, he just got chosen that night. As a doorman, I was always conscious about where my head was in relation to a brick wall, a good street fighter will quite happily ram your head back or to the side into the nearest brick wall, it saves him breaking his knuckles. If he gets it right, a clean knockout with life threating consequences could be the result so when you are in a potentially violent situation look for objects around you that could be used as a weapon against you, including brick walls.

Positions of attack and ambush

Never let your potential attacker dictate the battlefield if possible. Only go into areas you are familiar with or that you have researched beforehand if that area happens to be off the beaten track away from the crowds.

This is especially important for lone workers who may have to travel in downtown city urban areas late in the day or under darkness, always know alternative escape routes and have an exit strategy from the area should your situational awareness pick up on things that concern you. Trust your gut instinct.

Close up attack

Most confrontations start close, usually beginning with verbal assaults and progressing on to a physical level. When up this close remember the 5 Ds; (distance, dialogue, deception, distraction, and destruction). First thing to remember is distance if he is out of reach, you cannot be hit. You should never let someone you do not know into your personal space (punching or grabbing range), do not let people who you do not know get any nearer than 5 feet. Do not worry about looking stupid or being accused of being rude, it is far better than being beaten senseless and regretting that you were not more assertive in the first place.

If someone invades your personal space and refuses to back away, be prepared to get loud and shout or fight.

Getting yourself trapped or cornered

If someone corners you or puts you in a position where you are trapped, it is obvious that their intentions are sinister. Typical cornering can be something as simple as getting into your car in an indoor car park or getting your keys out in the front porch of your house.

A scuba diver is in more danger on the surface just before he can get on the boat or the last 100 feet of the surf breaks from a shark attack. Human predators follow the same instincts, they know when you are busy entering a property or car your mind gets switched off from the dangers around you and you are cut off from an escape route.

It is important when you visit shopping centre car parks, indoor or outdoor, that your situational awareness skills are fully switched on.

No matter how many times you have been there and are familiar with the territory don't let down your guard, especially when approaching your vehicle. Make sure you look all around you before you take out your keys or open your car boot as this is a feeding ground for the scumbag criminals and you are shopping so they know you probably have credit cards, valuables, cash or even keys for your car.

Places to steer clear of when parking the car. Corners of car parks with no escape routes, walking up dead-end roads with only walkways as a way out that you are not familiar with, flats with underground car parks without security gates and cameras.

The surprise attacks

Surprise attacks are exactly that; times and places you least expect them. They could be on the way back from a bar late at night or walking through a park in broad daylight but most surprise attacks are with the intention to mug you or sexually attack you.

Surprise attacks are normally instigated when you are separated from the herd, walking through the backend of town somebody jumping you from a shop doorway or behind a parked vehicle, again they are waiting in places where your guard will be down, usually after a night of going out on the town and they know your vulnerable from a few drinks and a late night.

Again, when you walk into parks make sure you are aware of all the exits and escape routes and stay near other people. Play your own mind game as if you were going to mug someone; where would you wait or hide?

If you are walking along a road with parked cars, make sure you observe long before you reach and the walk past any vehicle; is there anyone in there? H ow many are in there. If you are not comfortable or get a gut feeling zig zag and cross the road (dictate the battle ground)

(Important note if you get pulled into a car statistically you will not be seen again, so fight like your life depends on it)

Pincer movement by two attackers

Muggers and gangs often work in numbers so keep your eyes peeled for people in your vision suddenly moving apart and trying to look as if they do not know each other.

Always keep both within your sight and do not worry or be embarrassed about turning around and going back in the direction you came from. Again, it's times like these that you need to do everything in your power to stay near other people or escape routes.

When criminals work in twos one will normally distract you with a verbal conversation while the other moves in from your blind spots.

Earlier we talked about looking like a victim. If you look sharp and are practicing situational awareness, the chances are you will be looked over as a potential victim in the first place in favour of an easier target.

Surrounding by two or more attackers

Again, situational awareness is the most important thing, spot the trouble before it spots you. Taking on two or more assailants can mean you will be facing death or life changing injuries, do everything you can to get away without physical contact or a fight. I have had many fights working on the doors but when it involved multiples working on my own, I would use every verbal conflict management technique I could come up with, before engaging in physical violence.

It does not matter how much training you have had nor how many scenarios you have practiced if you are knocked to the ground in an attack by multiple assailants you are in big trouble. On the few occasions I have had to engage in physical fights with multiples if I am honest, my coming out unscathed was more down to luck and knowing where to position myself and the absolute refusal to go to the ground.

Probably one of the riskiest things that happened to me involving multiples was an interesting take on human nature, when a shark attacks a swimmer and people go into the water to attempt a rescue. On nearly all occasions the shark ignores the rescuers and continues to attack its original intended victim.

I was working a one-man door, it was near the end of the shift and there was a commotion going on outside the venue, there was one man with a bike being attacked by 5-6 well-built males. They were dressed as if they were probably builders and looked very strong and in good physical shape, the guy was on the ground and they were going for it, he was getting a right good kicking.

It's moments like this that you find out a lot about yourself, if these guys turned on me, I was as good as dead.

I ran into the road and pushed them out of the way and put myself as best I could between the man's head and the boots coming into try and kick it off. I was just waiting for the smash round the back of the head or being kicked in the back of the legs or grabbed and taken down, but it never happened. They just kept going for the intended victim and to this day I have no idea what it was about. The whole time they were pushing and barging me, but not once did they attack me and if they had, I probably would not have stood a chance.

Eventually I managed to drag this guy into the bar and out of harm's way. On another day or a different group of assailants, it might have been a different story and I consider myself lucky that it ended like it did.

I am not saying this is what you should do if you see someone getting attacked, I advise you to go and get help. It is more an anecdote on human nature.

Places to avoid

Places to avoid may not always be obvious

Car Parks

Try to stay out of underground car parks, these are perfect places for criminals and muggers and rapists to lurk, especially late at night when the clubs and pubs are shutting. Even during the day these places pose a risk because they have many blind spot areas that are not covered by CCTV whether it's a high-rise car park or underground car park, they are perfect mugging grounds or opportunist sexual attackers to drag you into a car.

Edges of the town centre

Most towns have a town centre and various venues, bars, and shops on the outskirts. Normally, in between, there are what I call suburban no man's land, the kind of place where the edge of the town centre finishes then maybe 1000 metres before you reach busier areas, again perfect hunting grounds for predators. These are normally areas where there are parks and houses and corner shops and many passageways leading off roads as short cuts to other areas, do not use them if possible, especially after dark.

Cash machines

Unless you are with a group of friends, never use cash machines in small shopping parades at night as this is a perfect place for criminals to wait for their potential prey. Even in town centres, be very wary of using a cash machine that is just around the corner of the high street even 15 metres off the beaten track makes you a potential target.

Public toilets

Many sexual attacks take place in public rest rooms, again if you are going to use a public toilet be sensible, do not use one in a park or quiet area of town such as a quiet parade of shops in the early evening or after dark. Go to a local bar, coffee shop or busy shopping centre.

Workplace carparks

Just because you know and are familiar of where you work does not mean it is safe. If you work late or arrive early, a work car park is much quieter than a public car park and can make a mugger or rapist feel as if he has more chance of success than out in a public area.

Looking through the eyes of a rapist.

No two attacks are ever the same but many sexual criminals' minds work the same way; one, they don't want to get caught and two, they want a victim that has the appearance of giving them the least trouble as possible. Most rapists want some sort of sexual fulfilment and gain a sense of power over their victim.

A group of rapists and sexual predators were interviewed in prison. Here is what the interviewer found out in terms of how they pick and approach their victims.

The first thing they look for is hair style, women with long hair get picked over women with short hair. The main reason for this is they prefer hair that can be grabbed and held onto easier. Women with short hair are not common targets.

Clothing comes into consideration as they will pick a woman who looks as if she has clothes that are easy to remove or rip off, some rapists even have scissors on them to cut off any difficult garments.

They will go for women who appear to be off guard, such as looking at a mobile phone, head in a handbag, unlocking a car or looking for keys.

Women are most likely to be attacked in a public car park, shopping centre, works car parks, garage compounds and restrooms. There is a good chance they may try and abduct you to a different location; this is a much more serious event and you could end up being raped and killed or at best, savagely beaten up.

Very few carried a weapon of any type due to the fact if they were to get caught, the prison sentence is a lot longer.

Any woman who puts up a fight would probably result in them deciding to leave it and go for an easier target. Anything that takes the attacker's time away is a big factor in aborting the attempted rape.

They would even probably be put off if a woman looked as if she were the type to put up a good fight.

These men also said they would be put off if any woman was carrying an item such as an umbrella.

If a woman sounded a personal attack alarm, they would abort the attack.

If you think someone is following you, make sure you let them know you are aware of them and make sure you look at them in the eye, the last thing they want is someone to be able to recognise them. Even engaging in conversation before they have made their move can be a big deterrent.

In the UK, unfortunately, you cannot carry Pepper spray but you can carry red dye spray. Again, most rapes are pre-meditated they are planned which means the adrenaline and heart rate will not be a big factor to the attacker before he attempts any sexual attack so if he has reasonable cognitive thinking, he's thinking about his escape from the situation afterwards. It makes sense to give him every reason to think his chances of getting away with it are getting slimmer by the second.

Most rapists said they would stop if a woman started yelling or shouted stop before the attack was physically started. When I teach women self-protection during the physical assault that I simulate with them, I make sure they keep shouting even while they are fighting back. It's not natural to be physical and shout at the same time so make sure however hard you are fighting back, shout and scream at the same time. This is extremely off putting to the attacker.

Overall, most rapists and sexual predators do not want grief or hassle from their intended victim. So, cause as much noise and fuss as possible and fight back like a woman possessed by the devil.

Safety when traveling in a car

Your situational awareness should start the minute you leave your house and close the front door. Some people leave very early for work when it's still dark so always be aware of criminals early in the morning waiting for a victim especially if you live in a secluded area or a flat with communal compound garages. An interesting statistic a high percentage of sexual attacks take place between 5.00 am and 8.00 am. This is the time you can be vulnerable with your head in the clouds thinking about the day ahead, maybe even half-awake which makes you less aware and an easier target.

Have your key ready long before you reach the car; if you are attacked you have a weapon plus you can enter the car quickly without having to fumble around in a bag or pockets. The minute you are inside the vehicle close the door and get into the habit of locking it.

Always make sure your mobile phone is fully charged both when leaving home and leaving work or any other time come to that.

In towns and cities, carjacking is becoming a regular occurring crime statistic, do not become a statistic. High risk areas are traffic lights T Junctions and car parks. If you are waiting and someone approaches the car, do not unlock the door or wind down the window. If you feel you must communicate, only wind down the window one or two inches so you can hear them. Even if a child approaches the car and asks, do not open the door. Criminals will use any means possible to distract you and get what they want. If you are hit from behind again do not just get out of the vehicle unless you feel it is safe to do so.

If you are driving late at night or in an unpopulated area during the day and you come across an accident, be cautious, do not just unlock and jump out of the car. Park in a safe spot slightly away from the scene keep your eyes peeled and call 911 or 999 on your mobile phone; only after you have called the emergency services should you leave the vehicle if you are 100% certain it's safe to do so.

If you think you are being followed, do not try and outrun the vehicle you believe to be following you or take lots of different turnings. Just head towards a more populated area such as a town or shopping centre where there are lots of people about. If you are still convinced you are being followed call the police, and, if possible, get the registration number. Whatever you do not drive home until you are sure you are not being followed.

When parking your car, pick a location that looks as if it's well-lit if you are going to be back later in the day. If it's a car park, steer clear of out the way corners or upper levels that will have very few cars in them later at night, a couple of cars on upper car park floors early is a great place for criminals to wait for a victim. If possible, always choose a car park with plenty of CCTV and a parking office. Make sure when you leave your car you remember what floor and its location. The last thing you want to be doing is wandering round a carpark late at night trying to find your car. Always make sure you park your car facing out of the parking space.

Do not leave valuables in your car while you are away from the car. If you cannot take them with you, put them in the boot out of sight. When you return to your car with key ready in your hand, survey the surrounding area and have a quick glance into the rear seat of the car just in case someone has got into your car to give you a nasty surprise.

Safety on public transport

Chances are. if you use public transport for work you know your stops and routes off by heart. If you are travelling on holiday or visiting a town or city you are not familiar with, make sure you know the stops the areas they go though. When I travelled New York City on public transport you can get on a bus or tube in a relatively safe area in lower Manhattan and within minutes be in the Bronx or the more sinister areas of Brooklyn. When travelling places like New York, London or other big cities, you must research the areas you will be travelling through if you want to stay safe. Make sure you know what time trains and buses stop running. The reason it is so important to know your routes, times and places is because the minute you start asking people for directions, you stand out as someone who does not know the area or city, perfect food for a predator.

Shopping malls and retail parks

Retail parks are convenient ways to shop and have a perception of safety about them, do not be fooled. Most retail parks are out of town and have a lot of empty space surrounding them. Car parks in out-of-town retail parks are a criminal's paradise, plenty of people with cars and money and goods. Plus, a perfect hunting ground for sexual predators and just like animals, they will hunt round the edges where they can quickly make a getaway or drag you into the undergrowth of surrounding fields or woodland.

Always park your car as near to the entrance to the shops and well-lit areas as possible. Do not park round the back or far away edges backing onto uninhabited environments beyond CCTV, security guards and other shoppers.

Avoid retail parks and malls after dark if you possibly can, remember security cameras and security guards are there to protect the retail outlets not you.

What makes out of town retail parks attractive to muggers and rapists is the fact there is a high proportion of women visiting them who have cash, credit card and jewellery on them, plus statistically women are less inclined to fight back.

As soon as you leave your vehicle walk a route to the entrance where you have a high visibility to other people, do not walk round the edges or in between cars, vans, or lorries.

Chances are you are more likely to be mugged on your way back to the car, you will have your hands full with shopping and probably fumbling around with your keys, perfect for someone who wants to take advantage. Hence park close to the entrance and if you cannot park near, stay on your guard and watch for anyone suspicious waiting about near your car or following you. If you notice someone do not hesitate to turn round and go back to the store and ask a security guard to escort you to the car, chances are they will only be to glad to help to relieve the boredom.

Jogging and outdoor exercise

Joggers, especially women, are the worst when it comes to personal security and safety. When you go out for a run leave your music player at home. This is perhaps the most dangerous weapon a rapist has to use against you and you loaded it. Music players take away all your senses and it leaves you unaware of the dangers of traffic and predators that lay in wait. To some sick individuals a woman running is a turn on, its predator verses prey.

When you go for a run always take a personal attack alarm with you. It's unbelievable that more women don't to carry these devices, they are cheap and easy to carry.

Never assume that running early morning or early evening makes you safer than any other time, rapists and muggers do not work 9-5 hours.

Avoid suburban off the beaten track pathways, they are convenient places for rapists to wait. Also, vary your route every time you go out. You may not see anyone when you are out running (especially if you have headphones on) but rest assured other people will see you and if the wrong person sees you on a regular basis running the same route, you are good victim potential.

Also don't put up your running route from your Fitbit on Facebook or other social media apps, you could be telling the wrong person where to attack you.

When you leave home always tell your partner or a member of your family the route you are going to be taking.

Dog walking

The same rules apply for people taking their dog for a walk or commercial dog walking businesses, situational awareness is essential. Commercial dog walkers need to be aware that many of the dogs they are given care of are worth a lot of money and will be considered an easy target by criminal gangs. Some dogs can be worth thousands of pounds, so knocking you over the head and doing you damage will not prick the conscience of criminal animal thieves.

There's no doubt in my mind even hardened criminals will be cautious about trying to steal an Alsatian, Rottweiler or one of the more aggressive breeds of dogs from you, but smaller breeds and traditional family pets will not deter criminal gangs looking to make money.

Animal theft is on the increase so dog walkers need to be fully alert when taking their pets into isolated country areas or parks. Unfortunately, commercial dog walking businesses usually have sign written vans which makes them stand out as easy targets for criminals so change your routes on a regular basis and try and stay near other dog walkers and people. I know this is hard as when I take the dogs out for a walk, I like being away from people and other dogs.

Here's a few steps you can take.

- The number one thing to do if possible is always have someone with you, never walk alone if you can help it.
- Carry a big stick
- Always keep your dog under control or on a lead.
- If you are walking along a footpath make sure you walk towards the oncoming traffic as this makes it far more difficult for opportunists to stop and attempt any criminal trying their luck
- If you are approached while walking your dog, always consider it may not be the dog they are after.
- Always inform someone where you are going and the route you take.
- Carry a personal attack alarm at all times, make sure you pull the pin and if the attacker comes for it, throw it. They are then left with two choices; find and stop the

alarm so you can run or keep coming at you but the alarm will keep going to draw attention to the situation.

- Same rules apply as if you were just walking about without a dog, do not walk your dog staring into a phone or going around with headphones on. It takes away all your vital senses.

ATM cash tills

ATMs are to thieves what honey pots are to bees. There are old school muggers and criminals and there is the new breed of criminal. The first one will punch or stab you for your money, the second will rob you with technology.

If possible, use a cash machine inside a bank, building society or shop. If this is not possible try and use one in an area where you are at least not on your own.

If you are using a cash till make sure you are aware of everyone around you, do not be embarrassed asking people to stay back as there are lines drawn so people do not stand right behind you. If you are in the middle of punching in pin numbers or sorting out a transaction and you get the feeling of someone being there who looks suspicious, just tap in the wrong number or cancel the request throw your hands in the air and swear, even look at the person as you do it. You have now made eye contact with a potential mugger you have also informed without saying a thing that you have no money in your account or at least can't get it out and you are pretty pissed off about it.

Now the ball is back in the potential mugger's court, is it worth trying to mug someone who has no money and is incredibly angry? Probably not.

Travelling & backpacking abroad without the knowledge of self-protection is like going to sea without a life jacket!

One of the most important factors in keeping safe while traveling anywhere in the world is situational awareness. But be aware, situational awareness will be completely different when walking the beaches of southern Australia to walking around the Bronx or Brooklyn New York. The beaches in south Australia are far safer than the Bronx, but on the other hand the Bronx will seem like a walk in the park compared to certain locations in South America or Africa. It is all relative.

It is worth remembering your wallet, camera and valuables are not worth dying for should you be forced to give them up.

Also remember 9 times out of 10 when you are selected by a predator for being robbed, that is all he or she will want and will quickly disappear once they have got what they want.

Then we have the other type of predator, the one who wants to sexually attack you, hurt you, kidnap you and maybe kill you to avoid any chance of you being a witness to their crimes against you.

- Be Aware never relax when in unknown territory.
- Constant awareness of your environment is your best defence. Always be alert, whether you are in your car, on the street, or accommodation.
- Always keep a rubber doorstop for when you stay in hotels, hostels and other types of accommodation. If someone tries to kick the door down or break in, it could give you vital seconds to get out of a window or alternative exit.
- Have a plan of action
- Play a mental "what if" game. Where would you go and what would you do should a dangerous situation occur?
- Trust your instincts
- Research shows that most assault victims had a feeling something was wrong just before they were attacked.
- Take notice; be aware if you are suddenly getting beautiful people paying unwanted attention to you.
- Keep your senses free. Do not wear radio headphones, large hats or other devices that make it difficult for you to sense an attacker. Always be alert.
- If you can afford a tracker GPS phone get one. (Keep extra batteries and charger units if you are planning any type of trip to the outback).
- Try and blend in, human predators are no different to predators in the animal kingdom, they will target group outsiders, people who look lost and are not in their normal environments

- Always have a plan, an exit route out of your accommodation in an emergency and when planning a walk through unknown territory, urban or bush, always look at places you can get help before you leave.
- Full First Aid kit and plenty of water especially when travelling in unpopulated areas.
- Always carry duct tape wherever you go, it has so many uses if you get a bad open cut or wound it's strong enough to close it up until you get proper medical attention. It can also be used as leg-splint, arm sling, repairing a cracked water bottle, butterfly bandage, temporary patch a hole in a canoe, hand cuff someone should the need arise, mend shoes and clothing, repair tents, you can even make a drinking cup from it, emergency repairs on a vehicle such as pipes and hoses, splint a broken tent pole and probably many other uses.

I am sure you have heard the saying stick to the road stay off the moors (American Werewolf in London) Sounds a safe way to travel. My own opinion is do not do what everyone else does. If back packers are abducted, chances are they were travelling along the side of a road. Predators do not go off the beaten track or wait in the woods on the off chance a hapless victim might come strolling by. Predators are always on the lookout for potential victims where potential victims are meant to be. If you are a travelling backpacker and on your own, you are bait for an opportunist predator.

Would you find a fisherman trying to catch a fish by a lake or sitting in the woods near a lake? I would personally say there is a good argument for not traveling by a roadside, you are too easy to spot and extremely easy to grab and be pulled into a car and abducted.

My advice would be travel just off the beaten track, I am talking maybe 25-50 feet away on an adjacent path or track if possible.

Where is the safest place to sit in a restaurant/café?

The main things to consider when taking a seat in a restaurant or café is the type of crime that could be committed while you are peacefully having a meal or coffee. The most probable crimes to be committed is robbery or terrorism.

Sit at a table where you can see the entrance, but not next to or close to the entrance. If possible do not corner yourself or your family, choose a seat where you can see the door but have an escape route through the back or at least access to a fire exit to the left or right so try not to box yourself in on a bench seat in corner.

Also keep far away from the area that takes the money and payments. If someone is going to rob the place this will be the focus point of any frustration and anger.

If it's not possible to sit with your back to the wall from the back of the room, position yourself left or right of the door but not close enough to attract attention and make it by a window because that way if a gun toting manic comes in, you have a chance of smashing through the window to make your escape.

When you are in a theatre, try and sit and the end of the aisles on the outside edges, preferably near an emergency exit sign.

Knives and edged weapons

Unfortunately, knives and edged weapons are becoming normal. All I am going to say is this, if you take someone on with a knife, chances are you are going to end up dead, it is as simple as that. Even a highly trained commando would not be stupid enough to take on someone with a knife, if there was an alternative course of action he could take. As I said earlier, if you have even the slightest suspicion that someone is carrying any type of weapon do not engage them, get away as quickly as you can, even if it means running away. I am not going any further into knife defence, because I personally do not believe there is any such thing. Trying to catch someone's arm or lock up their wrist whilst being stabbed at, is the equivalent of trying to commit suicide. If you find yourself in a situation up against a knife or bottle, pick up an object such as a bin, umbrella or bar stool and use it to keep distance and shout and scream for help.

The only techniques I teach students when it come to the knife is; if there is no other alternative, you have become cornered and there is nothing to put between you and the knife is basic blocking techniques that may, if you are really lucky enable you to get out of a corner or a dead end. Unfortunately, all this can do is give you a conscious decision on where you get cut or stabbed, rather than getting stabbed automatically in a vital organ.

If you have absolutely nothing to hand, keep your arms at 90 degrees in front of your vital points, with the palms of your hands facing inwards a cut to the outside of your arms. The bony part will be bad, but not as bad as if your palms were facing out exposing the soft flesh, tendons and veins of the inner side of the arms and wrists. Work your way out of the corner and run.

Knowing the signs of when someone is about to hit you

Remember the saying, it is the quiet ones you need to watch? Well in my experience it's true and here is why it's normally the case.

When someone gets angry and the adrenalin drop starts to kick in the conscious brain starts to shut down, this does not just happen to the victim it also applies to the attacker. If someone is screaming in your face, they are probably not at the stage of actually striking you, shouting in your face and splaying the arms out wide is body language, this person is saying to you I'm bigger than you, back down, get out of my space. This is your chance to do the sensible thing; step back make space use your fence (hands open palm above their hand height) and talk back calmly. You may feel like an idiot seeming to back down but do not think of it like that, you are hopefully ending a potentially violent confrontation.

On the other hand, if they are giving you 1000-yard stare and going pale in the face with fidgety hands and seem incapable of complex verbal communication, keep your distance and be prepared for fists to start flying.

The silence is caused by the rational brain being turned off by the primal brain (amygdala) and the blood is being pushed into the arms and legs, hence a pale face and twitchy hands. As the blood drains away from stomach and brain, getting ready for battle.

Some experienced nasty villains know this stuff and, when working the door, I would simulate the signs of my primal brain kicking in as a warning knowing certain individuals would be able to read my body language and demeanour. On the other hand, experienced street fighters are devious and sly and have learnt to disguise tell-tale signs of a pre-emptive strike.

The Law, two words you need to understand.

Reasonable and Necessary

When it comes to the law it would require far more information than I am qualified to give but if you can remember this, it should help keep you out of prison.

If you are forced to defend yourself and you must stop someone from doing you damage, was the force you used back against them reasonable and was it necessary?

If someone punches you in the face, then you punch them back in the face and they fall to the ground and you then proceed to stamp on their head, is that reasonable? The answer is obviously no. Was it necessary? Again no. If you had just punched them back and they had fallen to the ground, I would consider that reasonable and necessary for you to be able to get away from the scene to a place of safety.

If an attacker comes at you with a knife and you hit them with a bar stool and knock them out to stop yourself being killed, in my book that is reasonable force and was also necessary as your life was in danger. But if someone were shouting at you, took a swing and you picked up a chair and hit them round the head, the law would probably consider this as excessive force (unreasonable) and totally unnecessary.

Can you hit someone first? Pre-emptive strikes

There is no rule in law to say that a person must wait to be struck first before they can defend themselves.

If you believe you are in immediate danger and you need to use force to escape the situation, it is perfectly legal to do so. Even if someone does not retreat when being attacked, it is not evidence that they were not acting in self-defence.

Again, it may not feel good for the ego, always make sure you state in any police statements or in court that you genuinely feared for your safety and were scared and had to defend yourself in the manner you did because it was necessary for your safety.

If you feel sufficiently threatened you have the right to strike first; 9 times out of 10, the person who strikes first wins. I'm not ashamed to say nearly every fight I ever had on the door I hit first. My particular talent was knowing exactly when to do it so I was covered legally. If you get hit first, you are immediately put on the back foot and if you are hit hard enough you won't have time to recover and will be left to the mercy of your attacker and that prospect puts your life in danger.

Working the doors

I'm not going to go to deep into door work but I feel it needs to be covered for those who may want to do it as a career move to earn extra money. I could write a whole book on my 15 years working the doors, but for now, I will cover a few key points and a few of my experiences on my journey as a bouncer with some meandering advice to carry you through it more safely.

For 15 years I faced violence regularly on a Friday and Saturday night. I have worked on the frontline and behind the frontline of the battlefield. When I worked as a security officer in the casino, I was technically working behind the frontline. At the start of a shift I would brief the door team of anything important going on that night, what to look out for and to make sure the customer service was first class. Working as a doorman or security officer in a gaming establishment is completely different to working a bar or club. Casino managers do not want fights breaking out on the gaming floor or major players who might be spending 50k per night being upset or being forcibly kicked off the premises. Working in casinos is where I learnt all my conflict resolution skills. Management did not want security staff upsetting big players but at the same time I had to keep the peace and not let players with big egos take control of the gaming floor. The door team would also be kept on a tight leash unless it was necessary to bring them into the situation.

Then, on my weekends off, I would go off and work the clubs and bars where there would be fights or skirmishes most nights. It was like wearing two hats in the same industry. In the casino I had to play nice cop and, in the clubs, and bars, a not so nice cop.

If I am honest, when I started out working the doors I was in it for the thrill. he adrenaline rush was unbelievable and very addictive. I can remember plenty of nights rolling down the town centre steps or having a full out punch up with some 'Billy big bollocks' who thought he could take me on. The first five years I loved putting myself to the test and would even join other door staff who were watching over the taxi rank or food outlets after my shift for no extra pay, just for the chance of a bit more excitement for the night. Don't get me wrong I always looked on the job as being a protector of people, not a thug looking to hurt anyone. But if trouble reared its ugly head and the bad guys were trying to spoil people's nights out, I was always happy to oblige and deal with any situation. This may be difficult to understand for some people but I hate violence and violent people, I really detest it. However, at the same time I wanted to be able to confront and deal with it, and the only way to do that was to immerse myself into a world where the constant threat of aggression and violence existed. I wanted to understand violence within the eye of the storm and make myself confront and deal with it head on.

But after several years working behind the scenes at a casino and getting totally pissed off with managing unruly and aggressive door staff, I started to see things differently.

I started to realise it was far more fun and challenging to talk someone out of a fight rather than fighting them so I decided to study conflict resolution, rather than just physical conflict. When someone is shouting in your face and getting aggressive it makes all the difference as to how you react if they are spending 100k per month with the establishment or buying a pint of beer.

Working at the casino, we went through a lot of door staff. You had to go through a lot to get the right mix of doormen with the right temperament, not only did they have to have good conflict resolution skills but they also had to have the ability to walk the walk if it became necessary. On a team of four we would normally opt for what I called two Gucci doormen; good looking, smart and 'looked the part' guys and two battle-hardened old-school bruisers should things get ugly. I can remember one occasion having to have a quiet word with one of the door staff one night due to a complaint by a customer of being unnecessary manhandled down the stairway. After viewing the cameras the next day, I could see that this particular doorman was being heavy handed and probably trying to aggravate the situation so he could burn off some excess adrenaline. Anyway, after explaining to him that that kind of attitude would not be tolerated and exactly how the venue wanted altercations and disputes to be handled, a situation arose a few nights later where a regular customer had to be escorted off the premises by the same member of door staff. After the customer had gone, the doorman came into my office with a wide grin on his face and told me the guy had just tipped him £10 for being so nice escorting him out of the venue.

Working the doors really made me understand the word Karma, if you act like an arsehole working the door guess what you get in return? That's right, lots of arseholes trying to take you down.

My first five years on the door was a learning experience which covered real fighting, it was nothing like the movies or sparring down my kickboxing club, real fighting is ugly unfair and potentially life threatening to you and other people. Looking back, I put myself into some stupid situations. Although I never started trouble, I was always looking for it and most nights usually found it. Things luckily always turned out in my favour but now looking back, that was more luck than any super powered fighting skills.

After working at the casino and becoming a qualified conflict management and physical intervention trainer, my attitude changed. That was not the only thing that changed me. After witnessing so many acts of needless violence which included bricks, bottles, machetes and knives, it suddenly hit me how vulnerable I was, especially working one-man doors. Please understand this, you can't beat everyone you come up against unfortunately. So, my advice is to play the numbers game, the less fights you have, the more chance you have of not getting a beating off someone and his mates and ending up in A&E.

There were many things that I really hated and put my back up, one of them was doormen who cowered to the local big-time thugs, then took it out later on some poor drunk who had just had too much to drink and got a bit mouthy. Don't work the doors if you haven't got the balls to treat everyone the same, no matter what their reputation. Talk and treat everyone with respect, you should only get physical when there is no other alternative. Another pet hate of mine were door staff who gave it the 'big I am' working within a team but who didn't have the balls to work a one-man door.

I was lucky over the years; I got to work and learn with some really good teams of doormen who had my back and who I trusted with my life when the shit hit the fan.

If you decide to go and work the door, never judge a book by its cover, be it door staff you are working with or potential troublemakers. One night while talking to the door team at the casino one the regular members of the team was off and had been replaced by an older guy in his mid-fifties, an Aussie called Sam. Lovely guy, pleasant to talk to and came across as very polite. One of the younger guys turned to me out of ear shot and laughed under his breath and said "what's that old guy going to be able to do if it kicks off, what he didn't know was, I knew Sam really well and if this young newbie had used his observation skills, he would have noticed that Sam had hands like shovels, he wasn't that tall, but was stocky and made of pure thick bone and muscle. Also, what he didn't know was, I had trained with Sam. He was a Goju Ryu instructor who I had invited down to train at my martial arts academy, the first half the session he trained in what we were doing, the second half we got Sam to show us what he was all about. Let's just say I let him loose on doing hand and arm conditioning with my MMA fighting students and within 10 minutes they had had enough. Sam was as hard as nails and after seeing his Gojo ripping techniques, he would have probably ripped any attacker to shreds had he ever had reason to defend himself. I just turned to the questioning doormen and said let's hope it doesn't kick off then. So never judge a book by its cover on either side of the fence.

Over the years I got offered many bribes from drunken idiots to local drug dealers wanting to gain access to the club or bar. I was offered sums of twenty pounds to two hundred pounds some drunks even offered me their wallet. If you're going to work in bar and club security, make sure you are incorruptible. Remember why you are in the job in the first place, your job is to protect good people on a night out, from the bad people who live in the shadows preying off youngsters by offering them all sorts of dangerous substances and bad intent. If you take a bribe off a drug dealer, he then owns you and who knows where that may lead. Never in fifteen years did I ever take money from someone to enter a club or bar.

Working on the door you should be taking the moral high ground, looking after the bars' customers is your number one priority and making sure that no harm comes to them. Yes, there will be times when you might feel totally unappreciated, like the time I intervened and had to get physical with a guy kicking his girlfriend laying on the floor in a side street, only to help her up and have her push me away screaming 'leave him alone'; you just can't please everyone. On another occasion I got into a brutal fight with a drug dealer after he had punched a woman in the face. I got the guy into a corner and went to work. He then decided to run and I gave chase, eventually cornered him in a nearby car park and found myself joined by two other local door staff and police. The police handcuffed him and then came back to the bar to take witness statements. I had one police officer taking my statement while the other officer took a statement from the husband of the woman who had been hit. All I could hear was the husband saying yes, the guy had hit his wife but I don't know why the bouncer kept hitting him. Nothing like getting a thank you for defending and stopping an attack on his beloved.

Working the door can be a thankless task but like I said, always take the moral high ground and do the right thing, it's all that separates you from the predatory scumbags hiding and waiting in the shadows.

Not every event in the security industry is thankless, some people are extremely thankful. I can recall a very funny incident while working as a surveillance security officer in the casino. The door team called my office saying they were sure there were a couple having sex in the ladies toilets, so I went down to investigate.

I quietly entered the toilets with two other members of the door team and we listened outside the cubical door. Yep there was no doubt about it, there was a couple having a very good time so I knocked on the door and suddenly there was silence, I knocked again and basically said come on out, you have been rumbled so just come out. A couple of minutes later a male and female appeared very red faced both looking as if they had been dragged through a hedge backwards. Now the casino policy was immediate eviction from the casino for that sort of incident but I was not always one to follow the rules having been a bouncer for many years as well as a security officer I really only took dislike to people who were trying to punch my head off or obnoxious idiots who were being rude and threatening to me.

This couple were looking extremely sheepish and embarrassed but above all else they were polite and courteous. I can remember my words exactly, I said look I'm in a really good mood tonight so I'm going to pretend this hasn't happened but please don't come in here and do it again because next time I will have to ask you to leave and probably ban you. They were both nodding like crazy and repeating thank you, thank you, thank you. I finally said go back to the downstairs bar and enjoy the rest of your evening. The door team did give me a wondering look, as if to say 'why aren't you kicking them out?' From a personal point of view, I did not see it as a big deal. Now here's the funny bit, as we followed them in the direction of the bar, their respective partners got up and we realised that these two couples had gone out for the evening and one partner from each couple had decided on some different kind of fun on the side without their partners knowing. We were standing there gobsmacked and the look we were getting from the two we had just caught was priceless. They all quickly got up and proceeded to leave the premises with the male walking past me saying thanks mate, thanks mate, thanks. Now that was a very, very thankful customer because if I had kicked them out and filled in an incident form, that would have taken some explaining to both his and her partners.

Don't get tempted!

If you find yourself working within a door team that has been corrupted with any kind of drug dealing, get out and go and work somewhere else, the chances are it runs deep.

I know of door teams getting coked up in the club before opening. Have nothing to do with these types they are as bad as the rest of the predators and scumbags out there.

Working the door, the temptations are great especially for young doormen just starting out. There are drugs, bribes and girls and the last one will get you in as much trouble as the first two. Remember the story of Sampson and Delilah? Don't ask me why but girls are drawn to doormen, it must be something that goes back to cavemen times. Door staff are protectors and girls find that attractive. Sampson was strong and taking on the Roman empire until his mind was taken off the job by a woman called Delilah. If you get your mind taken off the job in a busy nightclub you and your team members will suffer for it. Your job is to watch the backs of your teammates and vice versa. There is a time and a place for everything; don't mix chatting up women and working the door together, it's a recipe for disaster.

As a doorman/bouncer understand one thing very quickly, that there are violent individuals out there that have no limits. Don't ever assume that the person in front of you thinks like you or has the same moral conduct as you. Do not ever think just because you wouldn't stamp on someone's head when they go down, that they will show you the same courtesy because the chances are, they won't.

Don't think the physical intervention training you received on your security course will be of any use to you because it won't. I am a qualified security trainer and I'm embarrassed by the skills I have to teach door staff and then expect them to keep themselves safe when working. The physical intervention techniques you are taught on your course would only be of any use if the person you were dealing with was so blind drunk they couldn't walk or see you, try getting an arm lock on a cocaine fuelled street fighter, good luck with that one, politically correct training will get you hurt.

Working in a team, it's easier to take control of someone in a safe way, but if you're working a one-man door and you have to get someone out of the bar and they don't want to go, you have a fight on your hands whether you like it or not.

Would I recommend learning martial arts for working the doors? Unless you have been doing it for years and studied different types the answer is definitely NO! If you want to get up to speed quickly enrol in your nearest boxing club, learn to hit and take a hit. My main martial arts are Karate and original Japanese Jujitsu (Gutter fighting) and boxing. I never really got around to martial arts like BJJ or Judo but I would highly recommend them because being able to get yourself up of the floor if someone takes you down is vital. One of the best doormen I knew was a Judo instructor, he used to hit people with planet earth as they say in Judo.

Another thing It's not just towns and cities that are dangerous places to work. Picturesque village bars and pubs can be far more dangerous and after my experiences I would say never work one-man doors out in the village sticks. I remember one evening being asked to cover a wine bar in a famous town/village near where I live. During the day it's normally full of locals and American tourists visiting tea shops and restaurants. I started the shift at 8pm supping on a cappuccino with a cool breeze in the air faced with a fantastic view of the local castle thinking 'what a result, this is going to be an easy number', little did I know. By 11 pm I was babysitting a gang of Hells Angels and most of the local gypsy community and the landlord decided for it to be a lock in until 2 am. In these situations, you have to play smart you have to get the right people on your side. It just so happened that the leader of the bikers came up to me and made it clear that if there was any trouble, he and his boys had my back. And true to his word when things ever got heated, he was there backing me up just in case. Like I said before, you can't fight everyone when you work one-man doors, you have to make relationships quickly and get locals on your side, I later learnt that most other door staff after one shift had refused to do it again. I did it for three months and asked for more money, as I felt the venue was not worth the risk for what I was getting paid, needless to say the venue refused to pay any more, so I left. Within 2 weeks of leaving a doorman was bottled in the face. Always trust your gut. I had worked some of the roughest shitholes around but this venue bar in a nice little quiet part of rural England gave me bad vibes.

When you first start out as a bouncer try and work within a night club, that way you will hopefully have an experienced team and a head doorman to show you the ropes. Working within a team is totally different to working a one-man door. I have done both and I can tell you now working a one-man door is not for the faint hearted but getting into an established door team is not easy. Most door teams are tight knit and like working with familiar and proven colleagues and don't like having to trust newbie doorman to back them up when it all kicks off. So, the minute you get your badge there's a good chance you will be chucked into the deep end on a one-man door, which could be a local bar or takeaway kebab house. If you are really lucky, you might get a partner to work on the taxi rank. When I started out, I started one a one-man door of an over 21s bar and then straight on to the taxi rank after. The best way of describing my first weekend, working the doors it was like a scene from Mad Max; fights in the taxi queue, fights in the takeaway opposite, fires in shop doorways keeping the homeless warm then finishing off the night running across rooftops after villains who had broken into the local department store. I loved every minute of it. But on a more serious note, be careful, when working one-man doors in the more secluded parts of town with no other door staff nearby to help you out. If the shit hits the fan, don't rely on the police to be there to help, well not in time anyway.

Shotguns and bullshitters

Another thing to watch out for on the doors are bullshitters. They will start chatting to you, naming names and telling you about local villains they are friendly with and who they have beaten in fights.

Nine times out of ten they are full of shit and are trying to see your reaction so they can decide if you are going to fight or fold should they push their luck with you. I have had idiots with no teeth telling me they are good fighters and pointing to their lack of teeth as some type of proof. I can tell you now I have had hundreds of fights and confrontations never did I lose any teeth so he must have been pretty bad at fighting. He also said he was coming back with a shotgun, chances are he wasn't going to, but you never know! So, stay alert especially at the end of your shift when you might have to walk a distance to your car.

Another thing, don't park your car close to the venue you are working or you might need new tyres and a paint job on a regular basis.

When you start out, especially if you are shoved onto a one-man door, it's easy to become a believer in the rubbish you get told and let people and reputations get in your head. Many occasion I had altercations with villains with a reputation, without knowing that they had reputations until someone else told after the event.

Remember one thing, whoever is standing in front of you, they are flesh and bone the same as you. The only difference is mindset. If they are prepared to go to more violent extremes than you and don't care about any consequences of their actions, you have to be able to match it because if you can't the day will come when you will be in a world of trouble.

I have seen many people (especially since the SIA brought in the licence) start working the doors thinking it's a bit of easy money. You might be lucky for a number of weeks depending where you are working but as sure as night turns to day, the time will come when you have to earn all those weekends of so-called easy money in one night and if you're not up to it, you can get seriously hurt.

Working as a doorman I can tell you now, you can never be seen to back down or you are finished in so many ways. Once you have backed down, they know they can do what they like and they will, give them respect by all means but never back down. That's why when a confrontation starts you need good conflict management skills, you can't de-escalate a situation if the vocal conversation starts at boiling point. If you work in a team and back down or don't step up to the plate when it kicks off physically, chances are you will never work again, in that area anyway.

We had an incident in the casino where two on duty doormen backed down to a coked-up thug and local villain with his mate on a roulette table, which led to a casino manager being attacked while they stood back and did nothing. That particular incident had being brewing for 20 minutes and should have been dealt with and nipped in the bud straight away but the two doormen had slowly been boiled with hot bullshit and once the villains saw fear, they knew they could do what they wanted. I was not on duty that night in the security room so I was watching all this unfold on camera the next day. The company that supplied the door staff were immediately fired. The two door staff never worked again in that town, other doormen actually threatened to walk off the job when they turned up at another venue to work if they were not replaced. When you have other doormen saying they would prefer to work on their own at a venue than with you, that's when you know you have fucked up big time.

So, if you really want to go in to door security, make sure you are prepared to face up to any threat because somewhere along the line you will have to face up to real thugs and villains, not just paper tigers.

Protests and civil unrest

2020 has been a year of a viral pandemic and worldwide protests. I will not get into the politics of why I believe this is happening but there are things you need to know if you are in the vicinity of a protest or thinking of attending one.

We all have the right to free speech and to be able to protest in a peaceful way on issues that we feel strongly about. But nine times out of ten at any large demonstration or protest, there will be an infiltration by an element of people with bad intent of hijacking it for their own agenda.

Recently there has been a multiple stabbing incident in Reading in the UK. This incident happened in a park after a large protest. People are saying it's not connected but that's not strictly true because without the event to hide behind, it would be very difficult to find something to hide behind to carry out a more sinister intention. Three people killed and another nine wounded, it's been classified as a terrorist incident according to the mainstream news.

In the US you have large protests with mobs storming congress in Washington resulting in 4 people ending up dead. You will always be at risk if you attend these events because there will always be individuals or organisations outside of the original protest movement who will infiltrate and cause as much violence and mayhem as possible. This applies to both right and left on the political landscape.

If you look at most violent incidents that happen at any mass gatherings there are three types of attack; the terrorist, lone wolf or small sleeper cell, commercial anarchists (gangs) and an individual with a grudge against society who wants to take it out as many people as possible.

The terrorist; anyone who commits murder or violence with a political agenda. For me it doesn't matter if they are working on his own with no upline command, working from their bedroom at home or living with mum or dad, they are a terrorist.

Terrorist cells; lone wolf and sleeper cells are the most dangerous of all, their whole objective is to cause as much death and destruction as possible and they know they will probably get caught or die in the process but don't care. If you and your family are in their sights, you are probably going to end up seriously injured or at worst dead.

In these dangerous times attending organised crowded events, protest, marches, pop concerts, crowded streets or major sporting events, you are at risk.

The commercial anarchists, (Gangs) these people latch on to protests and start fights and encourage destruction of property so they can make money from looting. These gangs are extremely organised and even have a pecking order working with other gangs within the community on who gets what shops and who is allowed to go in first.

These people are usually only dangerous if you get in their way and prevent them from their objective of gaining their commercial loot. They know if they can cause a big enough riot the police will stand back and they can get on with their objective. My advice is when you see this happening is don't be a hero; get out of the area as quickly as possible as these people will carry all types of weapons and if you stand between them and what they want chances are, they will do whatever it takes to get you out of their way.

Another thing to remember about riot situations is this, if you are singled out for any reason by rival protestor it won't be just them that come after you, the rest will join in. If one starts kicking you down on the ground the chances are, they will be joined very quickly by others who will start kicking you as well without even knowing or caring why you are being kicked in the first place. Crowds are extremely dangerous when the pack mentality kicks in.

There is no doubt we are living in unprecedented times. On the streets there is an air of menace that certainly wasn't there until recently. There is also a huge amount of underlying anger in the general population; morals and the ability to know what is right or wrong, moral conduct and doing the right thing seem to be on life support at this moment in history. I have never known a time when people seem so polarised against each other.

In the United States Police are being randomly attacked or shot at, often resulting in Police deaths. People moan about the police being sometimes brutal but I guess when you have a population that is armed to the teeth you can't blame them for being twitchy and sometimes overreacting.

In the UK there are now far more people being shot or stabbed then there ever used to be.

You may tell yourself things will get better but in reality, things usually only slowly and progressively get worse. I can't tell you what the answer is, I can only advise you on how to protect yourself and your loved ones.

Protecting your teenage children

When children become teenagers and eventually start going out to bars and clubs, they are going to meet lots of different types of people. Some good, some not so good and some who are nothing short of evil.

There will be lots of temptations for them to resist, it could be anything from taking drugs to being offered easy money to run with drugs and eventually become dealers themselves. When you are in your late teens a drug run can seem like easy money but once they get into the company of dealers and criminals it's very hard for them to get out again.

There were many occasions when I worked the doors in pubs and clubs I would notice a female who seemed to be under the influence of something far stronger than alcohol or weed. Turned out quite a few of them had been spiked. On a number of occasions, I even used their phone to contact parents and made them wait where I could see them until they were picked up. I always made a point of making sure someone was safe before letting them leave the premises if I was aware of a problem. Unfortunately, this is not common practice especially in busy nightclubs, security staff don't have the time to deal with type of problem.

Most towns now have street pastors who are contactable by door staff. If available they will always come to the rescue.

Make sure you tell your children about these risks, not talking about it will put them more at risk and don't worry about that look they give you when you tell them, they will take it in. It's not cool to look as if you are taking notice of your parents.

When children are in their late teens especially in times like these, it's easy for them to feel lost and directionless, this is when they are most vulnerable to being taken advantage of by criminals and see it as something glamorous.

I personally know first-hand young people who have become caught in the trap of being involved in the drugs trade. You may say it's their fault for doing it in the first place, but would you say that if it was your son or daughter? Young people need to be guided and mentored so they choose the right thing to do when offered a poison chalice.

This is where it's important to have role models earlier on in their life. I may have criticized some traditional martial arts as a self-protection system but as for providing good moral leadership and mentoring, it can't be faulted. If you find a good traditional martial arts school with an instructor who teaches respect, keeps good discipline, and provides moral guidance its worth every penny and could save you a lot of worry when they get older.

The point I'm trying to get across is this, you won't be able to stop your children coming into contact with bad people, it's impossible, what you can do is pre-arm them with the tools to make the right moves and decisions when they do come into contact with them.

What to do if you child hangs out with the wrong people

There's an old saying 'birds of a feather flock together'. It's easy for teenagers to fall into a group they feel accepted in, maybe they suffer from low self-esteem, are just not doing well at school and feel they are not worthy of being accepted by the type of friends you would find more to your taste for company. The most important thing to a teenager is to be, and feel accepted by, a group of other teenagers. It doesn't matter if they are good or bad, acceptance is all that matters in many cases.

The rule of 7. It's a fact that you, and people in general, are the average of the 7 people you hang out with. So, if your child hangs out with people who take drugs or steal, chances are they will eventually be doing the same. You won't be able to decide who your kids hang out with, it's impossible. My advice is this; as busy as parents are in a modern world, give them positive interests outside of school such as sports clubs and creative interest groups. If, from an early age, you give your children creative challenges that attract the type of youngsters who are not interested in the streets, you will be half way there. Encourage your children to take up an interest that takes time to develop and is as far away from instant gratification as possible. Drink, drugs and petty crime are objects of instant gratification. In other words, it requires no self-discipline and perseverance to obtain an emotional fix from it.

As a child, I had an upbringing that gave me a good idea of what was right or wrong and what was the acceptable way to behave. I remember clearly having a best friend at school who was an OK guy and when we left school we got up to all sorts of stuff, not bad or evil stuff, just stuff my parents would certainly not have approved of. Then he started mixing with another group of lads, who were definitely on the wrong side of the law. He pulled up in his car one day and I got in and saw he had a full tank of petrol and lots of, let's say, goodies in the back of the car. I asked him where it had come from and he openly admitted they had all been out the night before, stealing petrol and breaking into cars. That was the last time I went out with him, I automatically gravitated to other friends, I instinctively knew that was the line in the sand I would not cross.

If, and when, concerns come about who your teenager is mixing with, discussion and a civil conversation will be better than a shouting match that pushes them further into the clutches of undesirables.

Talk to them in an open and civil way, they may give off the impression they are not listening and don't care what you have to say,

 but most will go away and think about what you have said and absorb what you have tried to get across. If any teenagers are reading this, your parents are only saying what they are saying because they care about you. Drug dealers' dodgy friends and criminals do not have your best interests in mind.

TELL ME WHO YOUR FRIENDS ARE AND I WILL TELL YOU WHO YOU ARE OR WHO YOU ARE LIKLEY TO TURN OUT LIKE.

Give them your idea of boundaries, not ultimatums and get agreement of them. Don't push their friends away, whatever you may think of them. Keep your children's friends close and keep your children's potential enemies even closer.

You may not like it but while your teenager is developing, you will have to play the long game. Don't push them away, always have their best interests at heart and be open to conversation and chances are they will always stick close to home. Don't put them into impossible positions of not being able to approach you over concerns and forcing them further away making them even more vulnerable to outside influences.

Observe them from a distance and give them the freedom to move about freely with the privacy they need.

Teaching respect

If you don't talk to children with respect, how do you expect them to give it back and talk to you about their problems. If you act like an overgrown child, what's that saying to them?

If your child makes a mistake or does something wrong show them the same respect that you would show a waitress in a restaurant who had brought you the wrong order, I'm sure you wouldn't shout at them and say 'get me what I ordered you idiot!' I see this all the time in supermarkets when busy parents want their children to listen.

Respect has to come from within, it can't be forced or demanded.

Don't shout and yell, it teaches them nothing. When you have to correct your child's behaviour, make sure you talk calmly and you are directly in front of them making eye contact and explain why there's a problem.

Make sure you ask them why they are acting this way. Nine times out of ten it's because they are angry over not getting something or getting their own way. Simply take the time to explain why they can't have what they want or do what they want. But, stay calm.

Your child will do things differently to you to get the same outcome, don't tell them they are wrong or stupid or they will take offence and probably do something they really didn't want to do in the first place just to spite you.

What to do if your teenage children are being bullied

This is a very emotional subject. One of my most sought-after classes are my anti- bullying classes. If your children are being bullied on a regular basis, it can make you want to do things to others that would get you put away for life. I know what my instinctive reaction would be if one of my children were being bullied. It would be to go to war with the parents of the other child. But unfortunately, it's not that simple unless you like prison food.

If it's happening at school, your first port of call should be the school and the head teacher and don't be fobbed off with 'we will deal with it'. On a couple of occasions when my eldest had a few problems with a particular school bully, I visited the school and had a meeting with the head of the school. To my surprise I had to listen to ten minutes of the head teacher explain to me that the boy doing the bullying had issues and I needed to understand why it was going on.

As you can imagine this just started my blood boiling. There was me trying to sort out the fact my son was being tormented and made miserable at school, only to be told I should be sympathetic to the bully causing the problems. Trust me, this is not an unusual attitude for schools to take, many people including teachers opt for the easy politicly correct option because their hands are tied by rules and regulations.

I can't tell you what to do, I can only tell you what I did. I was not going to let his problems affect my son and made it clear that under no circumstances would I allow this to continue and if push came to shove, I would take it up with the bully's parents on a personal level outside of the jurisdiction of the school. There was no way I was going to let this carry on and if the school didn't sort it, I would sort it myself by whatever means necessary.

If you sit back in these situations, nothing gets done. I'm not saying this is the way you should play it but from my perspective, it worked because my son was never touched or bothered again. You can have all the school talks you want about bullying, you can get special guests in to have chats with the kids but sometimes the bully only understands one language and the people who don't understand or don't want to understand that, are not living in the real world.

The only people who are in your children's corner when they are being bullied or their lives are being made miserable is you, the parent. Don't leave it to someone who's more interested in defending the school bullying policy and being politically correct, than what's really happening to your child. When it comes to your child, make sure there's no quarter given when it comes to their safety.

More often than not, if your child is being bullied in school there's a good chance they will encounter the same characters down the local park or recreational areas out of school. Most bullies are too cowardly to act out alone, normally they only have the courage when they are with mates and accomplices.

When I was growing up and got approached outside of school by scumbags and bullies, it was a fair fight one on one and no weapons. Today is a different story. I have had many victims of bullying and violent attacks in my classes and when they fell victim it wasn't one on one, it was normally three or four on to one. When they were attacked it included kicks to the head when they were on the ground. I have even looked up the profiles of their attackers on Facebook and their profile photo was them standing there with 4 other friends with balaclavas on and holding claw hammers, these kids are 13 years old.

I don't think I need to explain to you what the parents of these children were like, you can't negotiate with these types of parents they are to put it frankly, scum, and their children really couldn't have turned out any other way.

To be honest my only advice is this, when your children are outside of school you have a certain amount of control over where they go and chances are, if they have had problems they will know where these kids hang out and steer clear.

Whether your children have been bullied or not, my advice to every parent is to get your child enrolled in proper self-defence training. Martial arts training is fine but make sure the instructor also has good knowledge of real self-protection and mixes them both up in the classes. Also, the instructor should be well versed in teaching situational awareness aimed at young adults and teens and teach edged weapons awareness, When I say edged weapons awareness I mean just that, not how to fight with knives but being able to spot the behaviour traits of someone carrying a knife.

A good self-protection instructor will teach your children what to do if they are in a dangerous situation and give them the appropriate tools to give them a fighting chance to get out without being badly hurt. However, these skills must go hand in hand with situational awareness, conflict management and escape skills.

If you're thinking why does my child need self-protection skills, just ask why it's important for your child to learn to swim or have basic first aid skills. While on the subject of first aid, make sure your child does know first aid because if they or one of their friends is ever attacked and suffers a stab wound, it could be the difference between life and death.

Types of bullying

Bullying occurs in many different forms, with varying levels of severity, threat and intention.

- **Physical Bullying** – poking, slapping, pushing, hitting, kicking, beating up.

- **Verbal Bullying** – shouting, taunting, name-calling, insulting, threatening physical harm.

- **Relational Bullying** – excluding, spreading rumours, instigating others to hurt someone.

- **Cyberbullying** – Sending malicious messages or images by Internet or mobile phone.

Please understand bullying is not to be taken lightly, it has lasting effects and should not just be treated as part of growing up. I personally know of young innocent lives that have been left with life changing physical injuries due to bullying that has turned physical.

Learn to recognise the signs of Bullying.

Children and teenagers have many reasons for not telling adults or their parents about being bullied.

- **They feel ashamed of being bullied.**

- **They are afraid of retaliation or the consequences of outing their tormentors.**

- **They don't believe adults, or anyone, will take them seriously.**

- **They feel they should be able to deal with it themselves or they will be seen as weak or stupid.**

- **Children who are subjected to any form of abuse from adults will not trust adults to deal with their concerns.**

- **They have been told that "grassing" is not a cool thing to do and there will be retribution for doing so.**

There are many clues and signs that indicate you child is being bullied, these are a few things to watch out for.

- **Is reluctant or refuses to go to school.**

- Clams up when you mention their day at school and ask what they have been up to.

- Asks for some sort of change in a long-term routine, like taking the bus to school, or suddenly stops going to the local park with friends.

- Does not want to take part in after-school activities that they have previously enjoyed or play with old friends.

- Seems hungrier than usual after getting home from school – it might be a sign that he is unwilling to brave the cafeteria at lunchtime.

- Suddenly shows signs of constant physical distress such as headaches, stomach-aches or nausea.

- Fakes illness in order to avoid going to school.

- Performance in school (grades, homework, attendance) suddenly declines

- Change of behaviour, becoming more introvert, angry and wants to be left alone.

- Uncharacteristically uses bad language

- Shows significant behaviour change after computer time or phone texts.

- Starts asking for lifts to and from school without a clear explanation of why it is needed.

- **Has unexplained bruises or injuries.**

If you can't solve the bullying problem and it starts to become physical, make no hesitation in getting the police involved. If that doesn't work, take your child out of school until its resolved and put as much pressure on the school and local authorities as you can. Every school is required to keep your child safe (duty of care).

Again, I cannot emphasise this enough, it may be a rare occurrence but bullying can lead to long term psychological trauma and life changing physical disabilities and even death by the perpetrators or suicide.

Bottom line is this; trust your instincts, not the politically correct protocol of the school or local education authority. If you feel your child is in danger, act on it and take them out of the situation.

Have a zero tolerance when it comes to your child being bullied!

Which fighting systems are the best?

In short there isn't one that is the best. If you are just a good boxer, you will be a very bad boxer if you get take to the ground by a grappling expert. Every martial art or fighting system has its weaknesses and its strengths. I have studied

Karate for years; you could say it's my foundation. I have practiced it and fought with it for so long that I understand all its weaknesses. I have made it my mission to study as much as I can in all the other fighting arts to balance my lack of skills by practicing other arts, to make what I teach far more realistic and effective. For movement and speed, I practiced dirty boxing, for groundwork I studied Judo and Jujitsu. Luckily, the style of Karate I was brought up with from an early age was heavily influenced by Japanese Jujitsu (Jujutsu) which practiced many throws and take downs.

The proof is in the results. The most effective fighters in the world today are MMA fighters. The clue is in the title MIXED MARTIAL ARTS. If you want to be an effective fighter then study every art you can.

Martial arts have many benefits and are a lifetime study. For me personally, they have positively influenced a massive part of my life. I am just as passionate about martial arts training now as I was at 14 years of age. When I say traditional training is not always a realistic way to train to fight, I'm not putting it down in any way, I just approach the subject with total honesty. Traditional martial arts are great for fitness, building a strong body and just as importantly a strong mindset. The big advantage training in traditional arts is that it's a lifetime of all-round body training whereas most of the pure MMA fighters I have trained don't stick at it past their first fight or 12 months of training. It's just the same with boxing, only the few are dedicated enough to keep it up, the main reason being its tough on the body with constant injuries and most people have jobs and families to think about. Studying traditional martial arts is one small piece of the big jigsaw puzzle of combat sports.

When you study traditional martial arts, you can then decide in which direction you want to go in. You can leave it there and just study the art or go for adding on the sports aspect by studying kickboxing, MMA, or even traditional knockdown martial arts like Kyokushin Karate. Also, if you are reasonably young and fit, take up Thai boxing. Practicing this type of martial art will give you resilience and make you battle hardened and toughen up your mindset. When I started out, all the good traditional martial artists in karate, Kung Fu and Jujitsu also practiced Thai boxing or Western kick boxing, this gave you what just practicing the traditional arts couldn't, getting used to being hit and taking a good punch to the face.

Developing this type of mindset is not an easy thing to do. As I said earlier some people are just not that way inclined and not cut out for physical combat.

But. if you are reading this book and want to go deeper, I would suggest the study of real self-protection.

In this country. the self-protection aspect of martial arts was introduced by Geoff Thompson and Peter Consterdine in the early 90s, or should I say reintroduced after a long absence of the original concepts and fighting systems of Fairbairn–Sykes.

William Ewart Fairbairn and Eric Anthony Sykes were two British men who served with the Shanghai Municipal Police in

China before WW2. Their system was to the point and ruthless in execution, their methods were used by British commandos and other special forces during the Second World War. This system is now simply referred to by many simply as Combatives.

If you are serious about self-protection, study Combatives with a reputable instructor. Combatives is based around military and special forces combat systems and is more about mindset than just being a separate fighting system. It takes what works and marinates it together with a deadly mindset of doing whatever it takes to survive a violent encounter, using pure aggression and turning yourself into a mugger's nightmare, it will give you a predatory mindset that's even greater than your adversary. When I have trained with real self-protection instructors such as Lee Morrison, I quickly noticed two things that stood out; many of the techniques they taught were very similar to traditional martial arts techniques but they applied them in in a completely different way and with a hell of a lot more attitude and destruction. Also, the training environment was more like it was 40 years ago, uncomfortable, edgy and slightly intimidating. If I could sum up the objective of Combatives in a couple of words, it would be to go out to completely annihilate and destroy your attacker in the most efficient way possible.

Training with a good Combatives instructor will give you all the tools you need to survive both physically and mentally, if you want to be physically prepared for the street you need to train well outside your comfort zone.

Epilogue

I hope this book serves its purpose in helping you understand the harsh realities of being violently attacked. If you read this book and take in the information, it may one day save your life.

Not many people will want to go as far as I have in facing violent confrontations and taming the fear of extreme violence, I use the word tame rather than conquer as I don't believe you can ever conquer fear. Fear is a healthy necessity to keep you safe. Every night I worked on the doors I had fear, I just learned to control it.

I had my last violent encounter on the doors two years ago and I hope that I never have another fight or confrontation again in my life. I prefer now to teach children and teenagers conflict resolution, how to deal with bullying and stay safe when they start going out and come up against the more unsavoury characters in society.

Being confronted regularly by conflict and violence has given me a clear understanding of how to avoid it in the first place. I now have a built-in sensor of people who are simply not worth my time and effort and I go out of my way not to engage with them on any level whatsoever. Life is short don't waste it in bad company.

Negative people are infectious!

Studying martial arts and training as a conflict management and physical intervention instructor, combined with 15 years on the doors making self-protection work for real, has given me the complete toolbox should anyone decide they want to cause me or my family harm.

This book has the intention of making you become aware of your surroundings and of the people around you the minute you walk out the relative safety and comfort of your home. Never take your personal safety for granted.

Learning martial arts, boxing or any combat system come to that, requires you to step out of your comfort zone. Stepping out of your comfort zone is what makes you grow as a person. What could be better way to grow as a human being than to learn skills that help protect you, your family and loved ones?

Thank you for taking the time to read this book, I hope it helps keep you and the people you love safe.